Ravenscourt
B·O·O·K·S
Teacher's Guide

Discovery

Books 1-8

A Very Strange Place
Rebuilding Fun
The Roof of the World
Stonehenge: A Special Place
Shipwrecks and Their Secrets
Migrating Creatures Big and Small
The Prince and the Beggar
Swiss Family Robinson

McGraw Hill SRA

Columbus, OH

SRAonline.com

McGraw-Hill SRA

Copyright © 2008 by SRA/McGraw-Hill.

All rights reserved. No part of this publication may be reproduced or distributed in any form or by any means, or stored in a database or retrieval system, without the prior written consent of The McGraw-Hill Companies, Inc., including, but not limited to, network storage or transmission, or broadcast for distance learning.

Printed in the United States of America.

Send all inquiries to this address:
SRA/McGraw-Hill
4400 Easton Commons
Columbus, OH 43219

ISBN: 978-0-07-611311-8
MHID: 0-07-611311-6

3 4 5 6 7 8 9 MAL 13 12 11 10

The McGraw-Hill Companies

Table of Contents

Ravenscourt Books 1
Reading and Fluency 2
Using *Ravenscourt Books* 3
Individual Progress Chart 8
Fluency Graph 9
Book Summaries 10
A Very Strange Place 12
    Answer Key 22
Rebuilding Fun 24
    Answer Key 34
The Roof of the World 36
    Answer Key 46
Stonehenge: A Special Place 48
    Answer Key 58
Shipwrecks and Their Secrets 60
    Answer Key 70
Migrating Creatures Big and Small 72
    Answer Key 82
The Prince and the Beggar 84
    Answer Key 94
Swiss Family Robinson 96
    Answer Key 106
Graphic Organizers 108

Ravenscourt Books

Placing Students

Written for middle school to young adult readers, **Ravenscourt Books** provides materials and activities for enhancing the comprehension and fluency of struggling readers. Each of these fiction and nonfiction selections is

- organized within themes that are both engaging and informative.
- built to provide students with additional opportunities to read independently.
- designed to provide frequent opportunities for reading to improve fluency and overall reading achievement.

Some teachers have found these selections align with the independent reading levels of students in the **Corrective Reading** program. Use the chart below to place your students in the appropriate set of **Ravenscourt Readers**.

	For students who have successfully completed	Reading level	Page count (average number of words per book)
Getting Started	Corrective Reading Decoding A*	1	28 (800)
Discovery	Corrective Reading Comprehension A*	2	28 (1,800)
Anything's Possible	Corrective Reading Decoding B1*	2	28 (1,800)
The Unexpected	Corrective Reading Comprehension B1*	2	28 (1,800)
Express Yourself	Corrective Reading Decoding B2*	3	44 (4,200)
Overcoming Adversity	Corrective Reading Comprehension B2*	3	44 (4,200)
Moving Forward	Corrective Reading Decoding C* Lesson 60	5	60 (7,500)
Reaching Goals	Corrective Reading Comprehension C* Lesson 60	5	60 (7,500)

*or have attained comparable skills

Components

The **Using Ravenscourt Books** section explains how to incorporate these components into an effective supplemental reading program.

Chapter Books
- Include eight age-appropriate books in each set
- Feature fiction, nonfiction, and retold classics
- Present additional practice for essential vocabulary and decoding skills
- Provide fast-moving story lines for independent reading

Fluency Audio CDs
- Model pronunciation, phrasing, intonation, and expression
- Assist students in improving their oral-reading fluency

Evaluation and Tracking Software
- Motivates students by delivering activities electronically
- Scores, records, and tracks student progress

Teacher's Guides
- Outline ways to use the series in your classroom
- Include comprehension activities, word lists, and fluency practice
- Provide prereading activities and postreading writing activities
- Address reading and language arts standards

Online Support

Go to **SRAonline.com** and click on **Ravenscourt Books** for additional support and materials.

Discovery

Reading and Fluency

Reading

Reading is not simply decoding or word recognition; it is understanding the text. Students who read slowly or hesitantly are not able to concentrate on meaning.

Fluency

Fluency bridges the gap between decoding and comprehension and characterizes proficient reading. Increased oral-reading fluency improves reading comprehension.

Fluent and Nonfluent Readers

The chart below presents an easy way to compare fluent and nonfluent readers. If students have several of the listed characteristics of nonfluent readers, refer to the sections on *Assessing Fluency* and *Fluency Practice* in the **Using *Ravenscourt Books*** section that begins on page 3.

A Fluent Reader	A Nonfluent Reader
Reads words accurately	Reads with omissions, pauses, mispronunciations, insertions, and substitutions
Decodes automatically	Reverses word order
Reads smoothly	Reads word-by-word, focusing on words
Reads at an appropriate rate	Reads slowly, hesitantly
Reads with expression and phrasing	Reads without expression; ignores punctuation
Reads with understanding of text	Reads with limited comprehension
Reads so text sounds like speech	Reads without natural intonation

Oral-Reading Fluency

Oral-reading fluency is the ability to read accurately, at an appropriate rate, and with good expression and phrasing. The foundation for oral-reading fluency is automatic word recognition and extensive practice with materials that are easy for the students to read.

Oral-reading fluency develops as a result of multiple opportunities to practice reading successfully. The primary strategy for developing oral-reading fluency is to provide extensive and frequent opportunities for students to read text with high levels of accuracy. This means that selected passages should be ones the students are able to read with at least 95 percent accuracy.

Repeated and monitored oral reading is an effective intervention strategy for students who do not read fluently. By reading the same passage a number of times, students become familiar with the words it contains and recognize the words automatically. This improves reading fluency and overall reading achievement. It also builds confidence and motivation—particularly when students chart their progress.

The minimum target oral-reading fluency rate is 60 *words read correctly per minute* (wcpm) for **Getting Started** and **Discovery**, 90 wcpm for **Anything's Possible** and **The Unexpected**, 130 wcpm for **Express Yourself** and **Overcoming Adversity**, and 150 wcpm for **Moving Forward** and **Reaching Goals**.

How to assess fluency, how to set realistic target rates, and how to practice fluency will be discussed in greater detail in the **Using *Ravenscourt Books*** section.

Using Ravenscourt Books

Grouping

Students who have completed *Comprehension A* will have mastered the decoding skills and vocabulary necessary to independently read the stories in **Discovery**.

Ravenscourt Books may be taught to the whole class, small groups, or pairs. Assign each student to a partner. Partners can do paired readings for fluency practice. The partners will read the same story at the same time. ***Ravenscourt Books*** may also be used for individual student reading.

Scheduling

Ravenscourt Books is intended to be used as a supplement to your core program and should be scheduled in addition to the regular lessons. Times to use the books include

- reading and language arts blocks,
- before- and after-school programs,
- summer school,
- and out-of-school reading with parental support.

A Suggested Lesson Plan for *Ravenscourt Books*

Part 1	1) Introduce the series, and help students select a book. 2) Assess students' initial oral-reading fluency by completing a "cold read" of one of the book's fluency passages. The **Fluency Passage** section can be found after the **Thinking and Writing** section for each book. (See *Assessing Fluency* on page 4.) 3) Have students complete the **Building Background** activities.
Part 2	1) Preteach the unfamiliar words for the first chapter in the **Word Lists** section of the *Teacher's Guide* for each book. 2) Have students read the title of the first chapter aloud. 3) Have students listen to a fluent reader read the first chapter as they follow along with the text. 4) Have student pairs take turns reading the chapter again. 5) Have students take the **Chapter Quiz.** 6) Have some students do repeated readings to improve oral-reading fluency. 7) Repeat Part 2 for subsequent chapters.
Part 3	1) Have students complete the **Thinking and Writing** section. 2) Take fluency scores, using the same fluency passage used in Part 1. Have students enter their scores on their **Fluency Graph.**

Selecting Books

The books in each set are leveled so students can start with any book in the set. However, students generally find contemporary fiction easier to read than nonfiction and retold classics. On pages 10–11 you will find **Book Summaries** that give a brief outline of each book.

- If the book is a retold classic, information about the original author is included.
- If the book is a good tool for teaching a literary term, the term is explained. The teacher should teach the term before the students begin reading.
- The last section includes other resources—books, films, or Web sites—that contain related information. These resources can be used for extra credit, reports, projects, and so on. Evaluate all books, films, and Web sites to confirm appropriateness of the content prior to sharing these materials with students.

Discovery

Using Ravenscourt Books

Introducing the Series

1. Write the series theme on the board.
   - Tell the students that the books in the set all relate in some way to this common theme.
   - Brainstorm ideas about the theme, and write the students' ideas on a large sheet of chart paper. Include words, topics, and types of stories related to the theme. Post this list for student reference.
2. The books in each set represent several genres—fiction, nonfiction, biography, science fiction, historical fiction, retold classics, and so on.
   - Ask the students to read the title and the summary on the back of the book they chose.
   - Have the students predict how their book relates to the theme.
   - If the book is nonfiction, ask the student to predict what kinds of questions it could answer.

Whole-Class Instruction

The following sections are designed for whole-class instruction but may be modified for small groups or individual instruction.

Set up classes in the *Evaluation and Tracking Software,* or make a copy of the **Individual Progress Chart** for each student.

Assessing Fluency

Make a class set of copies of the **Fluency Graph** on page 9 of the *Teacher's Guide.* Follow these steps to ASSESS STUDENTS' INITIAL ORAL-READING FLUENCY.

1. Have the student read a passage that is set at the appropriate length (60–150 words) and at the appropriate instructional reading level (at least 95 percent accuracy).
   - The **Fluency Passage** section can be found after the **Thinking and Writing** section for each book.
2. Ask the student to do a one-minute reading of the unrehearsed passage.
3. Ask the student whether she or he is ready.
   - Then say: **Please begin.**
4. Follow along as the student reads.
   - When an error occurs, mark the error.
   - Count the following as errors: mispronunciations, omissions, substitutions, insertions, and failure to identify a word within three seconds.
   - Don't mark words the student self-corrects.
   - Don't mark off for proper nouns.
5. At the end of one minute, make a vertical line on the page after the last word read.
6. Count the number of words up to the last word read.
7. Subtract the number of errors to determine the wcpm.
8. Enter the number of words read correctly on the student's **Fluency Graph** by filling in the column to the appropriate number.
9. At the bottom of the graph, circle the number of errors made.
10. Review any words the student missed and provide practice on those words. The minimum goals for fluency are the following:
    - The goal for students who have completed *Decoding A* or have equivalent skills is to read the books in **Getting Started** at a minimum rate of 60 wcpm.
    - The goal for students who have completed *Comprehension A* or have equivalent skills is to read the books in **Discovery** at a minimum rate of 60 wcpm.
    - The goal for students who have completed *Decoding B1* or have equivalent skills is to read the books in **Anything's Possible** at a minimum rate of 90 wcpm.
    - The goal for students who have completed *Comprehension B1* or have equivalent skills is to read the books in **The Unexpected** at a minimum rate of 90 wcpm.

Using Ravenscourt Books

- The goal for students who have completed *Decoding B2* or have equivalent skills is to read the books in **Express Yourself** at a minimum rate of 130 wcpm.
- The goal for students who have completed *Comprehension B2* or have equivalent skills is to read the books in **Overcoming Adversity** at a minimum rate of 130 wcpm.
- The goal for students who have completed Lesson 60 of *Decoding C* or have equivalent skills is to read the books in **Moving Forward** at a minimum rate of 150 wcpm.
- The goal for students who have completed Lesson 60 of *Comprehension C* or have equivalent skills is to read the books in **Reaching Goals** at a minimum rate of 150 wcpm.

Word Lists

Follow this procedure to preteach the words for each chapter of every book.

1. Provide students with a copy of the **Word Lists** page, or copy the words onto the board. Underline word parts if appropriate.
2. Begin with *Proper Nouns* by saying:
   - **These are the names of important people and places in Chapter 1.**
   - **Touch the first word in the column.**
   - Point to an underlined word part (if necessary) and say: **What sound?** (Signal.)
   - **What word?** (Signal.)
   - (Repeat until firm.)
3. For difficult and irregular words, say:
   - **Touch the word.**
   - **The word is ____.** (Signal.)
   - **What word?** (Signal.)
   - **Spell ____.** (Signal for each letter.)
   - **What word?** (Signal.)
   - (Repeat until firm.)

4. Follow the same procedure with *Unfamiliar Words*. Discuss the meanings of the words. Use the words in sentences as needed. The *Word Meanings* category is comprised of the words used in the *Word Meanings* section of **Building Background,** so some of the words may be familiar. Only use the following procedure for unfamiliar words.
   - Point to each unfamiliar word, say the word, and then say **What does ____ mean?** (Call on individual students.)
   - (Repeat until firm.)

Building Background

Use the **Building Background** section in the *Teacher's Guide* or on the *Evaluation and Tracking Software.* You can use this section as a whole-class activity or as an independent activity.

Whole-Class Activity

1. Divide the students into small groups. Hand out copies of the **Building Background** page for that book.
2. Read the questions in the *What You Know* section. Have the groups discuss the questions and write an answer for them. Have a member of each group read the group's answers to the class.
3. Read the words in the *Word Meanings* section.
   - Then read the directions and go over each question with the students and say, **Which word best answers this question?** (Call on individual students.)
   - Repeat this procedure for all of the words. (Note: If the directions indicate that the questions should be answered once the words have been introduced in the book, go over each word again after the students have read the word in context and have them answer the question associated with that word.)
4. Collect the papers and score them based on the number of correct answers. Refer to the **Answer Key** for each book.

Using *Ravenscourt* Books

Independent Activity

1. Hand out copies of the **Building Background** page. Have students take turns reading each question in the *What You Know* section. Have students write their answers before proceeding to the next question.
2. Have students read the words in the *Word Meanings* section. Then have them read the directions and complete the section.
   - When students are finished, collect the papers and score them based on completion and effort. Refer to the **Answer Key** for each book.

The teacher may enter the scores on the **Individual Progress Chart** found in the *Teacher's Guide* or on the *Evaluation and Tracking Software.*

Reading the Chapter

First, the students listen to a fluent reader read the chapter. The fluency model may be the teacher, a parent, a tutor, a teacher's aide, a peer, or the *Fluency Audio CDs.* Students read along, tracking the text with their fingers. Next, students take turns reading the chapter with their peer partner. An individual student reads aloud to the teacher, tutor, or parent, who gives feedback, points out missed words, and models, using punctuation, to improve expressive reading.

Chapter Quiz

After the second reading of the chapter, the student takes the **Chapter Quiz.** The quizzes have multiple-choice, true-or-false, sequence, and short-answer questions. The chapter quizzes are available on the *Evaluation and Tracking Software* or as blackline masters in the *Teacher's Guide.* Use the **Answer Keys** to score the blackline masters and enter scores on the **Individual Progress Chart** found on page 8. The *Evaluation and Tracking Software* will automatically grade and record the scores for all non-short-answer questions for each **Chapter Quiz.**

Students should take each quiz once and do their best the first time. Students must score a minimum of 80 percent to continue. If the student does not score 80 percent, he or she should reread the chapter before retaking the quiz.

Fluency Practice

Fluency practice improves comprehension. The teacher may choose different ways to practice fluency, depending on the student's needs. For students who are close to the target rate, have the student reread the whole chapter using one of these techniques:

- **Echo reading** A fluent reader reads a sentence aloud, and the student *echoes* it—repeats it with the same intonation and phrasing.
- **Unison or choral reading** A pair, group, or class reads a chapter aloud together.
- **Paired reading** The student reads a page aloud and receives feedback from his or her peer partner. Record the fluency scores on the **Fluency Graph** found in the *Teacher's Guide* or on the *Evaluation and Tracking Software.* Recording progress motivates student achievement.

For students who are significantly below the target rate, conduct **REPEATED READINGS TO IMPROVE ORAL-READING FLUENCY.** The student will reread the passages marked by asterisks in each of the books' chapters.

1. Set a target rate for the passage.
   - The target rate should be high enough to require the student to reread the passage several times.
   - A reasonable target rate is 40 percent higher than the baseline level.
   - For example, if the student initially reads the passage at a rate of 60 wcpm, the target rate for that passage would be 84 wcpm (**60** x .40 = 24; **60** + 24 = 84).

Using Ravenscourt Books

2. Have the student listen to the passage read fluently by a skilled reader or on the corresponding *Fluency Audio CD* while following along, pointing to the words as they are read.
3. After listening to the fluency model, have the student reread the same passage aloud for one minute.
    - A partner listens and records errors but does not interrupt the reader during the one-minute timed reading.
    - If the student makes more than six errors, he or she should listen to the fluency model again.
4. The student should read the same passage three to five times during the session or until the target rate is met, whichever comes first.
    - After each rereading, the student records the wcpm on his or her **Fluency Graph**.
    - If the target rate is not met, have the student read the same passage again the next day.
    - If the target rate is met, the student repeats the procedure with the next chapter.

Thinking and Writing

Many state assessments require students to produce extended writing about a story or an article they have read. Like **Building Background,** this section is not computer-scored and may be used in one of several ways. The *Think About It* section is intended to help students summarize what they have read and to relate the book to other books in the set, to the theme, or to the students' life experiences.

1. The questions in the *Think About It* section can be used for discussion.
    - Students discuss the questions in small groups and then write their individual responses on the blackline masters or using the *Evaluation and Tracking Software.*
    - The teacher may score the response using a variety of rubrics. For example, the teacher could give points for all reasonable responses in complete sentences that begin with a capital letter and end with appropriate punctuation.
2. For certain students, the teacher may ask the questions and prompt the student to give a thoughtful oral response.
3. Another option is to use *Think About It* as a mini-assessment. Have the students answer the questions independently on paper or using the *Evaluation and Tracking Software.*

The *Write About It* section gives students extended practice writing about what they have read. Students may write for as long as time allows.

The students may answer on the blackline master or use the *Evaluation and Tracking Software.* To motivate students, the *Evaluation and Tracking Software* includes a spelling checker and a variety of fonts and colors for students to choose from. This section is teacher-scored. Scores may be entered on a copy of the **Individual Progress Chart** or on the *Evaluation and Tracking Software.*

Students may keep their essays in a writing portfolio. At the end of the term students choose one of their essays to improve using the writing process. The final question in each *Write About It* section asks students to complete one of the graphic organizers that can be found as blackline masters in the back of this *Teacher's Guide* or on the *Evaluation and Tracking Software.* Graphic organizers are a structured, alternative writing experience. There are Book Report Forms, a What I Know/What I Learned Chart, a Sequencing Chart, and so on. Scores may be entered on the blackline master or *Evaluation and Tracking Software* version of the **Individual Progress Chart.**

Individual Progress Chart

Name: _____ Class: _____

- Enter the percentage correct score for each quiz or activity.

Book Title	Building Background	Chapter 1 Quiz	Chapter 2 Quiz	Chapter 3 Quiz	Chapter 4 Quiz	Chapter 5 Quiz	Chapter 6 Quiz	Thinking and Writing	Graphic Organizer
A Very Strange Place									
Rebuilding Fun									
The Roof of the World									
Stonehenge: A Special Place									
Shipwrecks and Their Secrets									
Migrating Creatures Big and Small									
The Prince and the Beggar									
Swiss Family Robinson									

Discovery

Fluency Graph

Name: _____ Class: _____

WCPM RATE
Number of words read correctly in one minute

Scale: 10, 20, 30, 40, 50, 60, 70, 80, 90, 100, 110, 120, 130, 140, 150, 160, 170, 180

Date

ERRORS: Above 6, 6, 5, 4, 3, 2, 1, 0

1. Read a fluency passage for one minute.
2. Find the next open column.
3. Color the column to the number that shows how far you read.
4. Mark the number of errors in the chart at the bottom.

Copyright © SRA/McGraw-Hill. Permission is granted to reproduce for classroom use.

Discovery

Book Summaries

A Very Strange Place
By Hilary MacAustin

Summary
This story tells about a young girl's first visit to an amusement park. The girl, named Lata, is from a village of small mud houses in a hot, dry place. She sees a world filled with trains that fly through the sky carrying shrieking people, spinning cups that make her dizzy, and other exciting and terrifying things. Lata first meets each marvel with terror, but by the end she is eagerly experiencing the wonders of this very strange place.

Literary Terms
Fiction: a piece of literature that is invented
Setting: the story environment; its time and place

Other Resources
Book: Winter, Jonah and Barry Blitt. *39 Apartments of Ludwig Van Beethoven* (Random House Children's Books, 2006)
Web site: http://fantasyfarm.org/

Rebuilding Fun
By Jennifer Weinstein

Summary
For their 12th birthday, twin sisters Rachel and Renata Billings receive tennis rackets from their grandmother. When the girls and their grandmother visit the local tennis court, they discover that time and neglect have made the court unusable. The girls decide to fix the tennis court. They figure out the supplies needed, calculate the cost, and begin raising funds. Their enthusiasm spreads, and what started as an idea from the two girls becomes a community project.

Literary Terms
Plot: sequence of events with rising action, conflict, climax, and resolution
Moral: the lesson a story teaches or implies

Other Resources
Book: Bunting, Eve and Ronald Himler. *Fly Away Home* (Clarion Books; Reissue edition, 1993)
Movie: *Full Court Miracle* (2003)
Web sites: http://www.kidscanmakeadifference.org/index.html
http://www.justgive.org/html/kidscorner/inspiringkids.html

The Roof of the World
By Elizabeth Laskey

Summary
When climber George Mallory was asked why he wanted to climb Mount Everest, he replied, "Because it's there!" The first few expeditions to the top of Mount Everest, including Mallory's, are the focus of this book. The author briefly describes the mountain's geography, topography, and climate. This is followed by a history of the first few Mount Everest expeditions. The book finishes with a report on the current status of Mount Everest and on the multiple climbs that are now attempted each year.

Literary Terms
Nonfiction: a factual piece of literature
Adventure: realistic characters and events; emphasizes action and suspense; setting is a real place or a place that could be real; sometimes includes a chase or attempt to find some object or reach a specific goal

Other Resources
Book: Jenkins, Steve. *The Top of the World: Climbing Mount Everest* (Houghton Mifflin, 1999)
Movie: *Everest* (1998)
Web sites: http://www.nationalgeographic.com/everest/
http://teacher.scholastic.com/activities/hillary/

Stonehenge: A Special Place
By Nancy J. Nielsen

Summary
Stonehenge, located in England, is a mysterious circle of large stones. People continue to speculate about how ancient peoples were able to move and place such large stones without the benefit of wheels or motors. People also continue to speculate about the purpose of Stonehenge. It may have been a type of calendar or a place of worship. Regardless of how it was formed or the purpose it served, it still draws visitors from around the world.

Literary Terms
Nonfiction: a factual piece of literature
Legend: a popular story, usually treated as historical fact but not verifiable

Other Resources
Book: Lynette, Rachel. *Stonehenge (Great Structures in History)* (KidHaven Press, 2004)
Movie: *Solstice at Stonehenge: 20th Anniversary* (2004)
Web sites: http://www.teachingtools.com/slinky/stonehenge.html
http://fun.familyeducation.com/outdoor-games/winter/35028.html

Book Summaries

Shipwrecks and Their Secrets

By Elizabeth Laskey

Summary

The ocean is littered with shipwrecks dating back to at least 1316 B.C. In 1982 divers discovered the ancient Uluburun wreck in what was once a busy trade route near Turkey. Divers have also found the wreckage of passenger ships from the mid 1800s. These wrecks contain treasure and historic links to the past. Scientists study recovered artifacts and ship engineering to learn why these ships sank. Modern technology has improved our ability to explore these secrets of the deep.

Literary Term

Nonfiction: a factual piece of literature

Other Resources

Books: Armstrong, Jennifer. *Shipwreck at the Bottom of the World: The Extraordinary True Story of Shackleton and the Endurance* (Crown Books for Young Readers; 1st Pbk. Ed edition, 2000); Platt, Richard and Duncan Cameron. *Shipwreck Detective* (DK CHILDREN; Bk&Acces edition, 2006)

Web site: http://www.seagrant.wisc.edu/madisonjason11/

Migrating Creatures Big and Small

By Jane Davin

Summary

Migration is a way for many animals to stay alive. Readers learn how six kinds of animals migrate: hummingbirds, sea turtles, loons, monarch butterflies, bison, and trout. There are different reasons why animals migrate. Some, like hummingbirds and monarchs, migrate to warmer climates before winter. Some, like sea turtles and trout, migrate to lay their eggs.

Literary Term

Nonfiction: a factual piece of literature

Other Resources

Books: Fowler, Allan. *Animals on the Move (Rookie Read-About Science)* (Children's Press, 2000); Pope, Joyce and Phil Weare. *Animal Journeys (Nature Club)* (Troll Communications, 1993)

Movies: *Born Free* (1966); *March of the Penguins* (2006)

Web sites: http://www.learner.org/jnorth/
http://animal.discovery.com/

The Prince and the Beggar

Retold by Nancy J. Nielsen

Summary

As a young boy, Tom Canty, who looks like Prince Edward Tutor, longs to meet a real prince. Through several unexpected events, Tom not only meets Prince Edward, but accidentally trades places with him. Although both boys try desperately to convince those around them that a mistake has been made, no one believes them. It is not until Tom is about to be crowned king that Edward, with Tom's help, is able to prove his true identity.

Author

After writing about his many travels in the western United States, Mark Twain finally gained fame throughout the world with stories about the innocent adventures of boys.

Literary Terms

Adventure: realistic characters and events; emphasizes action and suspense; setting is a real place or a place that could be real; sometimes includes a chase or attempt to find some object or reach a specific goal

Dialogue: the words spoken by characters in a story

Other Resources

Book: Dumas, Alexandre, Oliver Ho, Arthur Pober, and Jamel Akib. *Classic Starts: The Three Musketeers* (Sterling, 2007)

Movie: *The Chronicles of Narnia—The Lion, the Witch and the Wardrobe* (2005)

Web site: http://www.henrytudor.co.uk/page4.htm

Swiss Family Robinson

Retold by Jane Davin

Summary

The Robinson family is shipwrecked on a deserted island, which becomes their home. They build an elaborate tree house, and the sons make pets of various animals they find on the island. After ten years of fun and adventure, the oldest son, Fritz, discovers another person named Edward living on the island. Edward turns out to be Jenny, a young woman who pretended to be a man to stay safe. When a ship comes to the island, Fritz and Jenny leave to return to England.

Author

Swiss Family Robinson was written by Johann David Wyss (1743–1818). The manuscript was edited by his son, Johann Rudolf Wyss, a philosophy professor, librarian, and writer, who lived from 1782–1830.

Literary Term

Coming-of-Age Story: main character is initiated into adulthood through knowledge, experience, or both; changes may be from ignorance to knowledge, innocence to experience, false view of the world to correct view, idealism to realism, or immature responses to mature responses

Other Resources

Book: Ingle, Annie and Domenick D'Andrea. *Robin Hood* (*A Stepping Stone Book™*) (Random House Books for Young Readers; Reissue edition, 1991)

Movie: *Swiss Family Robinson* (Disney, 1960)

Web site: http://www.ciese.org/curriculum/shipproj/index.html

Discovery

Building Background

Name _____ Date _____

A Very Strange Place
What You Know

Write answers to these questions.

1. Think about the word *fun*. Write your own definition of *fun*. What are five things you call fun? Why are different things fun to different people?
   _____

2. Look up the words *industry* and *industrial* in a dictionary. Use the information to write a definition of *industrialized nation*. Name three industrialized nations. _____
   _____

3. Imagine that a child from a small village in a non-industrialized nation is visiting your house. List five things that would be strange or new to the child. _____
   _____

Word Meanings
Matching

Look for these words as you read your chapter book. When you find a word, draw a line to connect the word with the correct definition.

breath	to move from side to side in an unsteady way
color	close or firmly held
roller coaster	causing fear
scary	air that a person takes into the lungs and then lets back out
tight	what we see as a result of light waves being reflected off objects
wobble	a ride in an amusement park that has open cars moving on tracks that rise, curve, and drop in a sudden way

Word Lists

A Very Strange Place

Unfamiliar Words	Word Meanings	Proper Nouns	
metal place strange terrible	roller coaster	Aunty Lata Uncle	Chapter 1
empty touched worried	scary		Chapter 2
music race	color		Chapter 3
circle world	tight		Chapter 4
faces whole	wobbled		Chapter 5
flew	breath		Chapter 6

Discovery • Book 1

13

Chapter Quiz

Name _____ Date _____

A Very Strange Place
Chapter 1, "A Terrible Place"

Number the events in order from 1 to 5.

____ People getting off the train were not hurt or scared.

____ The air was full of strange smells.

____ The train was going too fast.

____ Lata saw a train track in the air.

____ A train stopped on the track.

Mark each statement *T* for true or *F* for false.

____ 1. The train track went up and down hills made of plastic.

____ 2. Lata yelled for someone to help the people on the train.

____ 3. Aunty said the roller coaster was safe.

____ 4. Lata wanted to try the roller coaster.

____ 5. Aunty said no one gets hurt on roller coasters.

Read the question, and write your answer.

What was the terrible place Lata was visiting? Why did she think it was terrible? _____

_____

_____

Chapter Quiz

Name _____ Date _____

A Very Strange Place
Chapter 2, "A Sticky Pink Cloud"

Mark each statement *T* for true or *F* for false.

____ 1. Lata and Grandmother came from a big city in another country.

____ 2. Lata and Grandmother were visiting Uncle and Aunty.

____ 3. The goats in Lata's village wore bells.

____ 4. Lata did not miss the smells from her village.

____ 5. In her village, Lata went barefoot.

____ 6. Grandmother was enjoying the park.

____ 7. When Lata saw the pink cloud, she was excited.

____ 8. Lata did not know what to do with the pink cloud.

____ 9. The pink cloud tasted like sweet air.

____ 10. Grandmother began to think the amusement park might not be so terrible.

Read the question, and write your answer.

What are four of the things this chapter tells you about Lata's village?

_____
_____
_____
_____

Discovery • Book 1

Chapter Quiz

Name _____ Date _____

A Very Strange Place
Chapter 3, "The Ride"

Fill in the bubble beside the answer for each question.

1. The animals on the ride
   - Ⓐ were on poles around a big wheel.
   - Ⓑ were painted with many colors.
   - Ⓒ both A and B

2. When it was their turn, Lata and Uncle
   - Ⓐ looked at each animal.
   - Ⓑ decided to ride tigers.
   - Ⓒ both A and B

3. As she rode, Lata
   - Ⓐ waved at Aunty and Grandmother.
   - Ⓑ leaned back and laughed.
   - Ⓒ both A and B

4. Lata rode with
   - Ⓐ Uncle and Grandmother.
   - Ⓑ Uncle and Aunty.
   - Ⓒ Aunty and Grandmother.

Read the question, and write your answer.

Why did Lata like the ride? _____

_____

_____

Chapter Quiz

Name _____ Date _____

A Very Strange Place
Chapter 4, "Turned Around"

Number the events in order from 1 to 5.

____ Uncle and Lata were running again.

____ Uncle stopped in front of big yellow cups.

____ People were sitting in the cups.

____ Lata did not think this ride would be fun.

____ The tiger ride was over.

Number the events in order from 6 to 10.

____ Lata laughed and waved at Aunty and Grandmother.

____ Lata and Uncle were laughing and yelling together.

____ Uncle pulled Lata into a big cup.

____ Lata's cup started turning faster and faster.

____ The cups started moving in a circle.

Read the question, and write your answer.

How do you know that Lata is beginning to like this strange place?

_____
_____
_____

Discovery • Book 1

Chapter Quiz

Name _____ Date _____

A Very Strange Place
Chapter 5, "The Whole World"

Mark each statement *T* for true or *F* for false.

_____ 1. After the ride, Lata was upset because she wobbled as she walked.

_____ 2. The next ride was for everyone but Grandmother.

_____ 3. This new ride was the strangest thing Lata had ever seen.

_____ 4. Grandmother looked scared, but Lata was excited.

_____ 5. Aunty had gone on the ride before.

_____ 6. Uncle sat with Grandmother and Lata sat with Aunty.

_____ 7. When Uncle told Grandmother the ride was safe, she began to relax and laugh.

_____ 8. From the top of the wheel, all the cars looked like ants.

_____ 9. Everything was so pretty that Lata forgot to be scared.

_____ 10. Lata was afraid because she could see so far away.

Read the question, and write your answer.

What did you learn about the world outside the park when Lata rode the Ferris wheel? _____

_____

_____

Chapter Quiz

Name _____ Date _____

A Very Strange Place
Chapter 6, "Flying"

Number the events in order from 1 to 5.

____ Lata decided to go on the flying ride.

____ Lata wanted to ride the roller coaster.

____ The family went to the flying ride.

____ Grandmother did not want Lata to go on the flying ride.

____ Lata loved flying.

Mark each statement *T* for true or *F* for false.

____ 1. Grandmother really liked riding the big wheel.

____ 2. Lata loved to swing.

____ 3. The swings on the ride were just like the swing in Lata's village.

____ 4. Lata screamed in fear on the flying ride.

____ 5. Lata said she loved flying.

Read the question, and write your answer.

Why was Lata ready to ride the roller coaster? _____

_____

_____

Discovery • Book 1

Thinking and Writing

Name _____ Date _____

A Very Strange Place
Think About It

Write about or give an oral presentation for each question.

1. How did Lata's idea of fun change during the story? _____
   _____

2. What things were familiar to Lata, even though they were different?
   _____
   _____

3. Where do you think Lata's village may be? Use what you know from the story to explain your answer. _____
   _____

4. What steps do you think Grandmother would take to fix a chicken and vegetable dinner in her village? How would it be different at Aunty's house? _____
   _____

Write About It

Choose one of the questions below. Write your answer on a sheet of paper.

1. Imagine you are Lata and you do one of the following: go to a football game, shop at a mall, or visit the airport. Use Lata's background and words to describe the things you see and what the people around you are doing.

2. Pretend Lata will visit you for your favorite holiday. Write a letter to her explaining what she will see and do.

3. Complete the Prediction/Outcome Chart for this book.

Fluency Passages

A Very Strange Place

Chapter 1 *page 2*

*Then Lata saw a train stop on the track. She watched the people sit in	15
the open train cars. They looked happy. The train went up a big hill. Then	30
it started to come down.	35
The train was going too fast. It could not stop! The people on the train	50
were screaming in fear. And the people on the ground* did not even care!	64
They were laughing and smiling. Why was no one helping the people on	77
the train?	79
"Someone help them!" Lata yelled. "Stop the train! Stop the train!"	90
She began to cry.	94

Chapter 6 *page 24*

*Grandmother did not like the big wheel very much. When she got	12
off the ride, she looked a little sick.	20
"No more flying," she muttered. "I like my feet on the ground."	32
"That's not flying," Uncle said. "There is another ride where you	43
really fly. Do you want to try it, Lata?"	52
Flying? It couldn't be. But Lata had never* dreamed she would ride	64
a tiger, or spin in a big cup, or sit at the top of the world!	80

- The target rate for **Discovery** is 60 wcpm. The asterisks (*) mark 60 words.
- Listen to the student read the passage. Count the number of words read in one minute and the number of errors.
- For the reading rate, subtract the number of errors from the total number of words read.
- Have students enter their scores on their **Fluency Graph.** See page 9.

Answer Key

Building Background

Name _____ Date _____

A Very Strange Place
What You Know

Write answers to these questions.

1. Think about the word *fun*. Write your own definition of *fun*. What are five things you call fun? Why are different things fun to different people? **Accept reasonable responses.**

2. Look up the words *industry* and *industrial* in a dictionary. Use the information to write a definition of *industrialized nation*. Name three industrialized nations. **a country where the people work in manufacturing and other businesses; accept reasonable responses**

3. Imagine that a child from a small village in a non-industrialized nation is visiting your house. List five things that would be strange or new to the child. **Answers will vary.**

Word Meanings
Matching

Look for these words as you read your chapter book. When you find a word, draw a line to connect the word with the correct definition.

- breath — air that a person takes into the lungs and then lets back out
- color — what we see as a result of light waves being reflected off objects
- roller coaster — a ride in an amusement park that has open cars moving on tracks that rise, curve, and drop in a sudden way
- scary — causing fear
- tight — close or firmly held
- wobble — to move from side to side in an unsteady way

12   Discovery • Book 1

A Very Strange Place

Chapter Quiz

Name _____ Date _____

A Very Strange Place
Chapter 1, "A Terrible Place"

Number the events in order from 1 to 5.

- **5** People getting off the train were not hurt or scared.
- **1** The air was full of strange smells.
- **4** The train was going too fast.
- **2** Lata saw a train track in the air.
- **3** A train stopped on the track.

Mark each statement *T* for true or *F* for false.

- **F** 1. The train track went up and down hills made of plastic.
- **T** 2. Lata yelled for someone to help the people on the train.
- **T** 3. Aunty said the roller coaster was safe.
- **F** 4. Lata wanted to try the roller coaster.
- **T** 5. Aunty said no one gets hurt on roller coasters.

Read the question, and write your answer.

What was the terrible place Lata was visiting? Why did she think it was terrible? **It was an amusement park. There were strange sounds and smells; there were loud noises; things were not where they should be.**

14   Discovery • Book 1

A Very Strange Place

Chapter Quiz

Name _____ Date _____

A Very Strange Place
Chapter 2, "A Sticky Pink Cloud"

Mark each statement *T* for true or *F* for false.

- **F** 1. Lata and Grandmother came from a big city in another country.
- **F** 2. Lata and Grandmother were visiting Uncle and Aunty.
- **T** 3. The goats in Lata's village wore bells.
- **F** 4. Lata did not miss the smells from her village.
- **T** 5. In her village, Lata went barefoot.
- **F** 6. Grandmother was enjoying the park.
- **F** 7. When Lata saw the pink cloud, she was excited.
- **T** 8. Lata did not know what to do with the pink cloud.
- **T** 9. The pink cloud tasted like sweet air.
- **T** 10. Grandmother began to think the amusement park might not be so terrible.

Read the question, and write your answer.

What are four of the things this chapter tells you about Lata's village? **Ideas: It was quiet and small; life was slower; the wind was hot and dry; houses were small and made of mud; there were goats in the village and the goats wore bells; people cooked over fires; it was far away.**

Discovery • Book 1   15

A Very Strange Place

Chapter Quiz

Name _____ Date _____

A Very Strange Place
Chapter 3, "The Ride"

Fill in the bubble beside the answer for each question.

1. The animals on the ride
   - Ⓐ were on poles around a big wheel.
   - Ⓑ were painted with many colors.
   - ● both A and B

2. When it was their turn, Lata and Uncle
   - ● looked at each animal.
   - Ⓑ decided to ride tigers.
   - Ⓒ both A and B

3. As she rode, Lata
   - Ⓐ waved at Aunty and Grandmother.
   - Ⓑ leaned back and laughed.
   - ● both A and B

4. Lata rode with
   - Ⓐ Uncle and Grandmother.
   - ● Uncle and Aunty.
   - Ⓒ Aunty and Grandmother.

Read the question, and write your answer.

Why did Lata like the ride? **The animals were pretty; the music was fun and happy; the animals went around and around; she could wave at her family; she felt safe; she could ride lots of different animals.**

16   Discovery • Book 1

A Very Strange Place

---

22   Discovery • Book 1

Answer Key

Chapter Quiz

Name _____ Date _____

A Very Strange Place
Chapter 4, "Turned Around"

Number the events in order from 1 to 5.

_2_ Uncle and Lata were running again.
_3_ Uncle stopped in front of big yellow cups.
_4_ People were sitting in the cups.
_5_ Lata did not think this ride would be fun.
_1_ The tiger ride was over.

Number the events in order from 6 to 10.

_8_ Lata laughed and waved at Aunty and Grandmother.
_10_ Lata and Uncle were laughing and yelling together.
_6_ Uncle pulled Lata into a big cup.
_9_ Lata's cup started turning faster and faster.
_7_ The cups started moving in a circle.

Read the question, and write your answer.

How do you know that Lata is beginning to like this strange place? **Ideas: She is trying new things; she is enjoying being dizzy; she is laughing with her uncle; she can't stop laughing.**

Discovery • Book 1   17

A Very Strange Place

Chapter Quiz

Name _____ Date _____

A Very Strange Place
Chapter 5, "The Whole World"

Mark each statement *T* for true or *F* for false.

_F_ 1. After the ride, Lata was upset because she wobbled as she walked.
_F_ 2. The next ride was for everyone but Grandmother.
_T_ 3. This new ride was the strangest thing Lata had ever seen.
_F_ 4. Grandmother looked scared, but Lata was excited.
_T_ 5. Aunty had gone on the ride before.
_T_ 6. Uncle sat with Grandmother and Lata sat with Aunty.
_T_ 7. When Uncle told Grandmother the ride was safe, she began to relax and laugh.
_F_ 8. From the top of the wheel, all the cars looked like ants.
_T_ 9. Everything was so pretty that Lata forgot to be scared.
_F_ 10. Lata was afraid because she could see so far away.

Read the question, and write your answer.

What did you learn about the world outside the park when Lata rode the Ferris wheel? **There were farms around the park, and they were green and pretty.**

18   Discovery • Book 1

A Very Strange Place

Chapter Quiz

Name _____ Date _____

A Very Strange Place
Chapter 6, "Flying"

Number the events in order from 1 to 5.

_3_ Lata decided to go on the flying ride.
_5_ Lata wanted to ride the roller coaster.
_1_ The family went to the flying ride.
_2_ Grandmother did not want Lata to go on the flying ride.
_4_ Lata loved flying.

Mark each statement *T* for true or *F* for false.

_F_ 1. Grandmother really liked riding the big wheel.
_T_ 2. Lata loved to swing.
_F_ 3. The swings on the ride were just like the swing in Lata's village.
_F_ 4. Lata screamed in fear on the flying ride.
_T_ 5. Lata said she loved flying.

Read the question, and write your answer.

Why was Lata ready to ride the roller coaster? **Ideas: She was getting over her fear of this strange place; she was learning to try new things; she was finding out that new things are fun.**

Discovery • Book 1   19

A Very Strange Place

Thinking and Writing

Name _____ Date _____

A Very Strange Place
Think About It

Write about or give an oral presentation for each question.

1. How did Lata's idea of fun change during the story? **Lata's idea of fun at the beginning was being back in her village. By the end, she had discovered that Uncle's idea of fun was not so bad. Her idea changed as she got over her fear and tried things one at a time.**
2. What things were familiar to Lata, even though they were different? **Ideas: the train, the tracks, clouds, animals and music, teacups, wheels, farms, swings**
3. Where do you think Lata's village may be? Use what you know from the story to explain your answer. **Ideas: She came from a desert area with hot, dry winds; homes were built of mud, not wood; the country was non-industrialized since the villagers cooked over fires and raised goats.**
4. What steps do you think Grandmother would take to fix a chicken and vegetable dinner in her village? How would it be different at Aunty's house? **Ideas: More time and work would be needed to buy or prepare the chicken, grow the vegetables, and cook over a fire in the village. At Aunty's house, she would be able to buy from the store and cook over a modern stove.**

Write About It

Choose one of the questions below. Write your answer on a sheet of paper.

1. Imagine you are Lata and you do one of the following: go to a football game, shop at a mall, or visit the airport. Use Lata's background and words to describe the things you see and what the people around you are doing.
2. Pretend Lata will visit you for your favorite holiday. Write a letter to her explaining what she will see and do.
3. Complete the Prediction/Outcome Chart for this book.

20   Discovery • Book 1

A Very Strange Place

Discovery • Book 1   23

Building Background

Name _____ Date _____

Rebuilding Fun
What You Know

Write answers to these questions.

1. Look up the following words: *campaign, goal,* and *plan.* How do these words fit together? _____
_____

2. If you wanted a skateboard park in your neighborhood, how would you find out what is needed to make one? List at least two ways to find out what you need to know. _____
_____

3. What is your favorite sport? Does it have established rules? Do you need a special place like a court or field to play the sport?
_____

4. Name three ways you could earn money to build a skateboard park. Which of them do you think would bring in the most money? Why?
_____

Word Meanings
Definitions

Look for these words as you read your chapter book. When you find one of these words, write its definition.

asphalt: _____

computer: _____

court: _____

freckle: _____

library: _____

success: _____

24   Discovery • Book 2

Word Lists

Rebuilding Fun

Unfamiliar Words	Word Meanings	Proper Nouns	
exactly excited kitchen rebuilding special tennis	freckle	Grandma Lorraine Rachel Renata	Chapter 1
choices suits younger	court		Chapter 2
build knew raise thought	library		Chapter 3
materials search surfaces wrote	computer		Chapter 4
concrete donations event friends fund-raiser group supplies	asphalt		Chapter 5
against	success	Channel Six Luis Morales Sam Carlson	Chapter 6

Discovery • Book 2

25

Chapter Quiz

Name _____ Date _____

Rebuilding Fun
Chapter 1, "The Birthday Gift"

Number the events in order from 1 to 5.

____ Rachel and Renata's parents put up balloons and streamers.

____ Rachel and Renata turned 12 years old.

____ The girls opened their presents from Grandma Lorraine.

____ Grandma Lorraine arrived.

____ The twins cut their birthday cake.

Mark each statement *T* for true or *F* for false.

____ 1. Rachel and Renata are identical twins.

____ 2. Grandma Lorraine brought two gift boxes and a cake.

____ 3. The girls always opened Grandma Lorraine's gifts first.

____ 4. Grandma Lorraine gave the girls silver tennis rackets.

____ 5. Grandma Lorraine was paying a friend to teach the girls to play tennis.

Read the question, and write your answer.

Why were Grandma Lorraine's gifts special? _____

_____

_____

Chapter Quiz

Name _____ Date _____

Rebuilding Fun
Chapter 2, "The Tennis Lesson"

Fill in the bubble beside the answer for each question.

1. How do you know that the girls were excited about their tennis lesson?
   - Ⓐ They got up early.
   - Ⓑ They ate eggs for breakfast.
   - Ⓒ They were almost ready when Grandma Lorraine got there.

2. Grandma Lorraine learned to play tennis because
   - Ⓐ it sounded like a fun game.
   - Ⓑ she liked sports and wanted to be part of a team.
   - Ⓒ she was good at it.

3. The tennis court was at the
   - Ⓐ middle school.
   - Ⓑ high school.
   - Ⓒ park.

4. What surprised the girls and their grandmother about the tennis court?
   - Ⓐ There was grass growing on the court.
   - Ⓑ There were cracks in the court.
   - Ⓒ Several people were waiting to play.

Read the question, and write your answer.

What do you think the girls and their grandmother will do next? _____

_____

Chapter Quiz

Name _____ Date _____

Rebuilding Fun
Chapter 3, "The Idea"

Mark each statement *T* for true or *F* for false.

____ 1. Rachel and Renata talked with their mother about the tennis court.

____ 2. The girls thought their father might know how to build a tennis court.

____ 3. Renata talked first because she was the youngest.

____ 4. Their father said they could find somewhere else to play.

____ 5. The girls wanted to build a new tennis court next to the old one.

____ 6. Their father said it would be easy to fix the tennis court.

____ 7. The girls asked their father to help.

____ 8. Their father said the girls should find out how a tennis court is made.

____ 9. Their father said he would help find out how much money they would need.

____ 10. Renata had some ideas for raising money.

Read the question, and write your answer.

By the time the girls went to bed, what work had they already started on their plan? _____

_____

_____

Chapter Quiz

Name _____ Date _____

Rebuilding Fun
Chapter 4, "The Plan"

Number the events in order from 1 to 5.

____ Mrs. Billings said the idea was fantastic.

____ Their father said he had told their mother about their idea.

____ Tim wanted to help too.

____ The girls got up in the morning and got dressed.

____ The family worked on a plan.

Mark each statement *T* for true or *F* for false.

____ 1. Renata said they would not need a new net.

____ 2. Mrs. Billings said the court should have a bench.

____ 3. Tim said they would need red paint for the lines.

____ 4. When they got to the library, the girls went to a computer.

Read the question, and write your answer.

How do you know that the whole family was excited about Rachel and Renata's idea? List at least three of the ways you know this.

_____

_____

_____

Discovery • Book 2   29

Chapter Quiz

Name _____ Date _____

Rebuilding Fun
Chapter 5, "Raising Money"

Number the events in order from 1 to 5.

____ The girls told their mother and father what they had found.

____ The girls went to their room to plan their first fund-raiser.

____ The girls thought concrete would be best for the tennis court.

____ Mr. Billings said he could help with the concrete.

____ Rachel and Renata were tired when they came home from the library.

Number the events in order from 6 to 10.

____ Some friends formed a babysitting club to raise money.

____ A man from the newspaper wanted to write a story about Rachel and Renata.

____ Many store owners gave the girls money to buy supplies.

____ Rachel and Renata organized a yard sale.

____ The girls and their friends had a bake sale.

Read the question, and write your answer.

Why do you think so many people helped Rachel and Renata raise money?

_____

_____

Chapter Quiz

Name _____ Date _____

Rebuilding Fun
Chapter 6, "Success!"

Mark each statement *T* for true or *F* for false.

_____ 1. The girls were excited to see the newspaper story.

_____ 2. The newspaper story said the girls had all the money they needed.

_____ 3. The girls cut out the story and put it in their scrapbook.

_____ 4. Tim said they could sell some of his toys to get more money.

_____ 5. The girls were excited about their new fund-raising ideas.

_____ 6. It was late afternoon when Grandma Lorraine called.

_____ 7. Grandma Lorraine was at the tennis court talking to two men.

_____ 8. The men were from Channel Six.

_____ 9. Channel Six promised to give as much money as the girls had already raised.

_____ 10. Within a week the new court was finished.

Read the question, and write your answer.

Do you think fixing the court or playing on it was the most fun for Rachel and Renata? _____

_____

Discovery • Book 2   31

Thinking and Writing

Name _____ Date _____

Rebuilding Fun
Think About It

Write about or give an oral presentation for each question.

1. Why does this story seem like it could really have happened?

   _____

   _____

2. How was the tennis court idea both a campaign and a goal?

   _____

   _____

3. Rachel and Renata did not just fix the tennis court. What else did they do? _____

4. Think about the title, *Rebuilding Fun*. This could have two meanings. What do you think was fun for the girls? Explain your answer.

   _____

Write About It

Choose one of the questions below. Write your answer on a sheet of paper.

1. Design a community project like the one Rachel and Renata had. Find out what you would need to do it. Plan your campaign. Explain how you would raise money to complete the project.

2. Pretend you are a newspaper reporter. Write an article about the tennis court project. Explain why the girls wanted to rebuild the tennis court, and tell how they made it happen.

3. Write a thank-you note from Rachel and Renata to Channel Six, thanking the station for its donation.

4. Complete the Problem → Solution → Effect Chart for this book.

Fluency Passages

Rebuilding Fun

Chapter 1 *page 2*

*The twins could hardly wait for the party to start. Their mom and	13
dad had put up balloons and streamers. Their six-year-old brother, Tim,	24
had made a banner. The banner said, "Happy 12th Birthday, Rachel and	36
Renata!" Their grandmother was bringing the cake.	43
At two o'clock their doorbell began ringing. Grandma Lorraine was	53
first. She came into the house with* two big gift boxes and the cake.	67
Rachel and Renata ran to help her.	74
"Thank you, girls," Grandma Lorraine said with a laugh. "I was	85
afraid I would drop that cake down the steps!"	94

Chapter 6 *page 24*

*The next morning Mr. Billings went to buy a paper. When he came	13
home, Rachel and Renata grabbed the paper from him. Then they ran to	26
the kitchen to read their story.	32
The man from the newspaper had called them after the yard sale to	45
find out how much money they had raised. At the end of the story he*	60
wrote, "For all their hard work, Rachel and Renata Billings still need 500	73
dollars to fix the tennis court." The girls were excited to be in the	87
newspaper.	88

- The target rate for **Discovery** is 60 wcpm. The asterisks (*) mark 60 words.

- Listen to the student read the passage. Count the number of words read in one minute and the number of errors.

- For the reading rate, subtract the number of errors from the total number of words read.

- Have students enter their scores on their **Fluency Graph.** See page 9.

Discovery • Book 2

Answer Key

Building Background

Name _____ Date _____

Rebuilding Fun
What You Know
Write answers to these questions.

1. Look up the following words: *campaign, goal,* and *plan.* How do these words fit together? **campaign: a series of planned actions carried out in order to reach a goal; goal: something that a person wants or works for; plan: a way to accomplish something. Accept reasonable responses.**

2. If you wanted a skateboard park in your neighborhood, how would you find out what is needed to make one? List at least two ways to find out what you need to know. **Ideas: Internet, library, skateboard magazines, other skateboard parks**

3. What is your favorite sport? Does it have established rules? Do you need a special place like a court or field to play the sport? **Accept reasonable responses.**

4. Name three ways you could earn money to build a skateboard park. Which of them do you think would bring in the most money? Why? **Answers will vary.**

Word Meanings
Definitions
Look for these words as you read your chapter book. When you find one of these words, write its definition.

asphalt: **a dark, sticky substance like tar that is mixed with sand or gravel and used mainly to pave roads**
computer: **an electronic machine for storing large amounts of information, performing calculations at very high speeds, or controlling the operation of other machines**
court: **a space that is marked out for playing certain games**
freckle: **a small brownish spot on the skin that is brought out on the face or arms, usually by exposure to the sun**
library: **a place where books, magazines, newspapers, records, and other materials are kept for reading or borrowing**
success: **the result that was hoped for**

Chapter Quiz

Name _____ Date _____

Rebuilding Fun
Chapter 1, "The Birthday Gift"
Number the events in order from 1 to 5.

2 Rachel and Renata's parents put up balloons and streamers.
1 Rachel and Renata turned 12 years old.
4 The girls opened their presents from Grandma Lorraine.
3 Grandma Lorraine arrived.
5 The twins cut their birthday cake.

Mark each statement *T* for true or *F* for false.

F 1. Rachel and Renata are identical twins.
T 2. Grandma Lorraine brought two gift boxes and a cake.
F 3. The girls always opened Grandma Lorraine's gifts first.
T 4. Grandma Lorraine gave the girls silver tennis rackets.
F 5. Grandma Lorraine was paying a friend to teach the girls to play tennis.

Read the question, and write your answer.

Why were Grandma Lorraine's gifts special? **Ideas: They were unusual; they showed a lot of thought; there was always more than just what was in the box.**

Chapter Quiz

Name _____ Date _____

Rebuilding Fun
Chapter 2, "The Tennis Lesson"
Fill in the bubble beside the answer for each question.

1. How do you know that the girls were excited about their tennis lesson?
   ● They got up early.
   Ⓑ They ate eggs for breakfast.
   Ⓒ They were almost ready when Grandma Lorraine got there.

2. Grandma Lorraine learned to play tennis because
   Ⓐ it sounded like a fun game.
   ● she liked sports and wanted to be part of a team.
   Ⓒ she was good at it.

3. The tennis court was at the
   Ⓐ middle school.
   Ⓑ high school.
   ● park.

4. What surprised the girls and their grandmother about the tennis court?
   Ⓐ There was grass growing on the court.
   ● There were cracks in the court.
   Ⓒ Several people were waiting to play.

Read the question, and write your answer.

What do you think the girls and their grandmother will do next? **Accept reasonable responses.**

Chapter Quiz

Name _____ Date _____

Rebuilding Fun
Chapter 3, "The Idea"
Mark each statement *T* for true or *F* for false.

F 1. Rachel and Renata talked with their mother about the tennis court.
T 2. The girls thought their father might know how to build a tennis court.
F 3. Renata talked first because she was the youngest.
T 4. Their father said they could find somewhere else to play.
F 5. The girls wanted to build a new tennis court next to the old one.
F 6. Their father said it would be easy to fix the tennis court.
T 7. The girls asked their father to help.
T 8. Their father said the girls should find out how a tennis court is made.
T 9. Their father said he would help find out how much money they would need.
T 10. Renata had some ideas for raising money.

Read the question, and write your answer.

By the time the girls went to bed, what work had they already started on their plan? **They had decided what they wanted to do, they had talked about it with their father, and they had planned what to do next.**

---

34   Discovery • Book 2

Answer Key

Chapter Quiz

Name _____ Date _____

Rebuilding Fun
Chapter 4, "The Plan"

Number the events in order from 1 to 5.

_3_ Mrs. Billings said the idea was fantastic.

_2_ Their father said he had told their mother about their idea.

_4_ Tim wanted to help too.

_1_ The girls got up in the morning and got dressed.

_5_ The family worked on a plan.

Mark each statement T for true or F for false.

_F_ 1. Renata said they would not need a new net.

_T_ 2. Mrs. Billings said the court should have a bench.

_F_ 3. Tim said they would need red paint for the lines.

_T_ 4. When they got to the library, the girls went to a computer.

Read the question, and write your answer.

How do you know that the whole family was excited about Rachel and Renata's idea? List at least three of the ways you know this.
Ideas: Everyone offered to help; the family planned together; everyone added ideas to the list; they thought of ways to raise money; they thought of who could help.

Discovery • Book 2   29

Chapter Quiz

Name _____ Date _____

Rebuilding Fun
Chapter 5, "Raising Money"

Number the events in order from 1 to 5.

_2_ The girls told their mother and father what they had found.

_5_ The girls went to their room to plan their first fund-raiser.

_3_ The girls thought concrete would be best for the tennis court.

_4_ Mr. Billings said he could help with the concrete.

_1_ Rachel and Renata were tired when they came home from the library.

Number the events in order from 6 to 10.

_8_ Some friends formed a babysitting club to raise money.

_10_ A man from the newspaper wanted to write a story about Rachel and Renata.

_6_ Many store owners gave the girls money to buy supplies.

_9_ Rachel and Renata organized a yard sale.

_7_ The girls and their friends had a bake sale.

Read the question, and write your answer.

Why do you think so many people helped Rachel and Renata raise money?
Ideas: good idea for the community; would be good to restore and renovate the park; girls were enthusiastic and determined

30   *Discovery • Book 2*

Chapter Quiz

Name _____ Date _____

Rebuilding Fun
Chapter 6, "Success!"

Mark each statement T for true or F for false.

_T_ 1. The girls were excited to see the newspaper story.

_F_ 2. The newspaper story said the girls had all the money they needed.

_F_ 3. The girls cut out the story and put it in their scrapbook.

_T_ 4. Tim said they could sell some of his toys to get more money.

_F_ 5. The girls were excited about their new fund-raising ideas.

_F_ 6. It was late afternoon when Grandma Lorraine called.

_T_ 7. Grandma Lorraine was at the tennis court talking to two men.

_T_ 8. The men were from Channel Six.

_F_ 9. Channel Six promised to give as much money as the girls had already raised.

_F_ 10. Within a week the new court was finished.

Read the question, and write your answer.

Do you think fixing the court or playing on it was the most fun for Rachel and Renata? **Accept reasonable responses.**

Discovery • Book 2   31

Thinking and Writing

Name _____ Date _____

Rebuilding Fun
Think About It

Write about or give an oral presentation for each question.

1. Why does this story seem like it could really have happened?
realistic scenario; girls developed a workable plan; girls did not do all the work themselves; girls had trouble raising money; people helped because they liked what the girls were doing

2. How was the tennis court idea both a campaign and a goal?
The girls made a plan and followed it through; they discussed it with their father and got permission; they researched and worked at ways to raise money to accomplish their goal.

3. Rachel and Renata did not just fix the tennis court. What else did they do? **Accept reasonable responses.**

4. Think about the title, *Rebuilding Fun*. This could have two meanings. What do you think was fun for the girls? Explain your answer.
Ideas: tennis court project; learning to play tennis at a court they had restored

Write About It

Choose one of the questions below. Write your answer on a sheet of paper.

1. Design a community project like the one Rachel and Renata had. Find out what you would need to do it. Plan your campaign. Explain how you would raise money to complete the project.

2. Pretend you are a newspaper reporter. Write an article about the tennis court project. Explain why the girls wanted to rebuild the tennis court, and tell how they made it happen.

3. Write a thank-you note from Rachel and Renata to Channel Six, thanking the station for its donation.

4. Complete the Problem → Solution → Effect Chart for this book.

32   *Discovery • Book 2*

Building Background

Name _____ Date _____

The Roof of the World
What You Know

Write answers to these questions.

1. Find Mount Everest on a world map. Is it north or south of the equator? What continent is it on? Which mountain chain is it in? Which two countries is it a part of? _____
   _____

2. Why do you think people enjoy mountain climbing?
   _____

3. What kind of equipment do you think would be needed to climb a mountain? _____
   _____

Word Meanings
Synonyms and Antonyms

Look for these words as you read your chapter book. When you find a word, write a synonym or antonym for the word.

Synonyms

area: _____

dangerous: _____

hidden: _____

Antonyms

above: _____

heroes: _____

true: _____

36   Discovery • Book 3

Word Lists

The Roof of the World

Unfamiliar Words	Word Meanings	Proper Nouns	
building mountain world	above	Mount Everest Nepal Tibet	Chapter 1
altitudes avalanche breathe chance climbers guides heavy oxygen summit wore	hidden	Andrew Irvine British George Mallory Noel Odell Sherpas [SHER-pahs]	Chapter 2
beehives crevasse edge forced gotten straw strong thrilled	dangerous	Edmund Hillary Khumbu Icefall [KHOOM-boo] New Zealand Tenzing Norgay [TEN-zing NOR-gay]	Chapter 3
crushed energy places	true		Chapter 4
knight medal raised thought	heroes	London Queen Elizabeth II	Chapter 5
period rules since	area	Peter	Chapter 6

Discovery • Book 3

Chapter Quiz

Name _____ Date _____

The Roof of the World
Chapter 1, "The Tallest Mountain"

Fill in the bubble beside the answer for each question.

1. How tall is Mount Everest?
   - Ⓐ more than 29,000 feet tall
   - Ⓑ 1,450 feet tall
   - Ⓒ as tall as the Sears Tower

2. What are the three sides of Mount Everest called?
   - Ⓐ the West Face, the South Face, and the Northeast Face
   - Ⓑ the Nepal Face, the Tibet Face, and the Nepal-Tibet Face
   - Ⓒ the North Face, the East Face, and the Southwest Face

3. What are the lower parts of Mount Everest like in spring and summer?
   - Ⓐ They are dry and barren.
   - Ⓑ They are cold, and the slopes are still covered with ice.
   - Ⓒ They are green and full of life.

4. What makes the upper regions of Mount Everest seem even colder than they are?
   - Ⓐ snow and ice
   - Ⓑ chilly winds
   - Ⓒ the lack of living things

Read the question, and write your answer.

Why do you think Mount Everest is called the "roof of the world"?

_____

_____

38   Discovery • Book 3

Chapter Quiz

Name _____ Date _____

The Roof of the World
Chapter 2, "'Because It's There'"

Number the events in order from 1 to 5.

____ George Mallory and Andrew Irvine climbed to 26,800 feet.

____ In 1922 a team of British climbers tried to climb Mount Everest.

____ Noel Odell saw two small dots near the top of Everest.

____ Mallory returned with another British team to try to climb Mount Everest.

____ A snowstorm came, hiding Mallory and Irvine from view.

Mark each statement *T* for true or *F* for false.

____ 1. The British paid Sherpas to be their guides.

____ 2. The first people to die on Everest were two British climbers.

____ 3. When asked why he wanted to climb Everest, Mallory said, "Because it's there!"

____ 4. Odell found the bodies of Mallory and Irvine.

____ 5. The bodies of Mallory and Irvine were discovered at the same time.

Read the question, and write your answer.

Why is it uncertain if Mallory and Irvine were the first climbers to reach the top of Mount Everest? _____

_____

_____

Discovery • Book 3

Chapter Quiz

Name _____ Date _____

The Roof of the World
Chapter 3, "Going Up"

Mark each statement *T* for true or *F* for false.

____ 1. Edmund Hillary was born in Australia in 1919.

____ 2. Hillary took care of sheep to train for climbing.

____ 3. In 1951 a British team invited Hillary to join them to try to climb Everest.

____ 4. One man on Hillary's team was a Sherpa named Tenzing Norgay.

____ 5. The team had ten climbers and 20 Sherpa guides.

____ 6. The team hiked 20 miles to get to the first camp on Everest.

____ 7. The team had maps to help guide them through the Khumbu Icefall.

____ 8. The Khumbu Icefall is made of big blocks of ice.

____ 9. Norgay saved Hillary's life when Hillary started to fall into a crevasse.

____ 10. The team made it from the Khumbu Icefall to the beginning of the Death Zone in about a week.

Read the question, and write your answer.

Why do climbers say Camp 8 is the beginning of the Death Zone?

_____
_____
_____

40   Discovery • Book 3

Chapter Quiz

Name _____ Date _____

The Roof of the World
Chapter 4, "The Push to the Top"

Number the events in order from 1 to 5.

____ On May 28, Hillary and Norgay started out as the second summit team.

____ At night the wind almost tossed Hillary and Norgay off the mountain.

____ At 27,900 feet, Hillary and Norgay stopped to camp.

____ Hillary and Norgay melted snow to make hot drinks and ate crackers.

____ The first summit team had to turn back because their oxygen had run too low.

Number the events in order from 6 to 10.

____ Hillary and Norgay started up to the summit at six thirty in the morning.

____ Hillary and Norgay made it to the top of Mount Everest.

____ Hillary and Norgay got up at four o'clock in the morning on May 29.

____ Hillary spotted a crack in the steep wall of rock.

____ Hillary had to "cook" his boots to thaw them enough to get them on.

Read the question, and write your answer.

How long did Hillary and Norgay remain on the summit? Why didn't they stay longer on the top of the mountain? _____

_____

_____

Discovery • Book 3

Chapter Quiz

Name _____ Date _____

The Roof of the World
Chapter 5, "Everest's Two Heroes"

Fill in the bubble beside the answer for each question.

1. Why did Norgay and Hillary look gloomy as they neared camp?
   - Ⓐ They had failed to reach the summit.
   - Ⓑ They were too tired to smile.
   - Ⓒ They thought their oxygen would run out before they made it safely down.

2. What did Queen Elizabeth II do for Hillary and Norgay?
   - Ⓐ She gave Norgay a medal and made Hillary a knight.
   - Ⓑ She gave them money to give to the Sherpa people.
   - Ⓒ She had newspaper photos of the two climbers taken and published.

3. Why does Hillary care deeply for the Sherpa people?
   - Ⓐ They are poor and need his help.
   - Ⓑ He admires their culture and traditional way of life.
   - Ⓒ He would most likely not have made it to the top of Everest without the help of Norgay and other Sherpas.

4. How has Hillary helped the Sherpa people?
   - Ⓐ He has encouraged banks to lend them money.
   - Ⓑ He has raised money to build schools and hospitals in Sherpa towns.
   - Ⓒ He has taught many Sherpas how to climb Mount Everest.

Read the question, and write your answer.

Why do you think Hillary and Norgay are considered heroes?

_____

_____

Chapter Quiz

Name _____ Date _____

The Roof of the World
Chapter 6, "Mount Everest Today"

Mark each statement *T* for true or *F* for false.

____ 1. In 1960 Hillary's son Peter climbed Mount Everest.

____ 2. More than 2,000 people have climbed to the top of Everest since 1953.

____ 3. Hillary thinks it is good that so many people are climbing Everest today.

____ 4. Climbers have left tents, oxygen tanks, ropes, and other trash on the mountain.

____ 5. Nepal is making new rules to help keep Everest clean.

____ 6. Climbers must now carry out all their trash and gear when they leave the mountain.

____ 7. Nepal made the area around Everest into a national park.

____ 8. Climbers can still cut down trees to use for cooking fires.

____ 9. It is dangerous for climbers to remain high on the mountain for too long.

____ 10. Many people still want to climb Mount Everest "because it's there."

Read the question, and write your answer.

Why won't Nepal cut back on the number of people it lets climb Everest each year? _____

_____

_____

Thinking and Writing

Name _____ Date _____

The Roof of the World
Think About It

Write about or give an oral presentation for each question.

1. Mallory claimed he wanted to climb Mount Everest "because it's there." What are some other reasons people climb mountains?
   _____
   _____

2. Why do you think climbers going up Mount Everest go in teams?
   _____

3. If Nepal decides to limit the number of people who climb Mount Everest, how should the country do it? _____
   _____

4. Would you ever climb a mountain? Why or why not? _____
   _____

Write About It

Choose one of the questions below. Write your answer on a sheet of paper.

1. Imagine that you are Odell watching Mallory and Irvine on their way up to the summit and then seeing them disappear behind the clouds. Write a description of the climbing scene and explain how you feel.

2. Write a newspaper article for *The London Times* about Hillary and Norgay's successful climb to the summit of Mount Everest.

3. Write an informational article about the importance and accomplishments of the Sherpa guides on Everest.

4. Complete the Main Idea/Details Chart for this book.

44   Discovery • Book 3

Fluency Passages

The Roof of the World

Chapter 2 *pages 4 and 5*

*People called "Sherpas" live in Nepal. They live near the slopes of	12
Mount Everest.	14
In the early 1900s, climbers from other parts of the world began to	27
think about climbing Mount Everest. No one had ever climbed it before.	39
In 1922 a British team of climbers went to Mount Everest.	50
The British team asked the Sherpas for help. The British* gave them	62
money to be their guides.	67
The climb is very hard. The climbers have to be roped together. If	80
one climber slips, the rope helps keep him or her from falling.	92

Chapter 5 *page 21*

*Norgay and Hillary reached some of the team the next day at a	13
camp far below the summit. At first the team thought Hillary and Norgay	26
had failed. The two men looked gloomy as they got near the camp. But	40
that was only because they were so tired. They were too tired to even	54
smile!	55
Norgay and Hillary's news hit* London the day Queen Elizabeth II	66
was crowned. But they got a bigger picture in the papers than she did!	80
They were heroes. Later they met the queen.	88

- The target rate for **Discovery** is 60 wcpm. The asterisks (*) mark 60 words.
- Listen to the student read the passage. Count the number of words read in one minute and the number of errors.
- For the reading rate, subtract the number of errors from the total number of words read.
- Have students enter their scores on their **Fluency Graph.** See page 9.

Discovery • Book 3

Answer Key

Building Background

Name _____ Date _____

The Roof of the World
What You Know

Write answers to these questions.

1. Find Mount Everest on a world map. Is it north or south of the equator? What continent is it on? Which mountain chain is it in? Which two countries is it a part of? **north of the equator; on continent of Asia, north of the subcontinent of India; part of the Himalayan mountain chain; Tibet and Nepal**

2. Why do you think people enjoy mountain climbing? **Ideas: adventure, challenge, thrill of accomplishment**

3. What kind of equipment do you think would be needed to climb a mountain? **Ideas: special boots, ropes, camping equipment**

Word Meanings
Synonyms and Antonyms

Look for these words as you read your chapter book. When you find a word, write a synonym or antonym for the word.

Synonyms

area: **region, zone**

dangerous: **perilous, unpredictable**

hidden: **concealed, out of sight**

Antonyms

above: **below, under**

heroes: **cowards, losers**

true: **false, fallacious**

36   Discovery • Book 3

The Roof of the World

Chapter Quiz

Name _____ Date _____

The Roof of the World
Chapter 1, "The Tallest Mountain"

Fill in the bubble beside the answer for each question.

1. How tall is Mount Everest?
   - ● more than 29,000 feet tall
   - Ⓑ 1,450 feet tall
   - Ⓒ as tall as the Sears Tower

2. What are the three sides of Mount Everest called?
   - Ⓐ the West Face, the South Face, and the Northeast Face
   - Ⓑ the Nepal Face, the Tibet Face, and the Nepal-Tibet Face
   - ● the North Face, the East Face, and the Southwest Face

3. What are the lower parts of Mount Everest like in spring and summer?
   - Ⓐ They are dry and barren.
   - Ⓑ They are cold, and the slopes are still covered with ice.
   - ● They are green and full of life.

4. What makes the upper regions of Mount Everest seem even colder than they are?
   - Ⓐ snow and ice
   - ● chilly winds
   - Ⓒ the lack of living things

Read the question, and write your answer.

Why do you think Mount Everest is called the "roof of the world"? **Ideas: It's the world's highest mountain; sea level is far below its top.**

38   Discovery • Book 3

The Roof of the World

Chapter Quiz

Name _____ Date _____

The Roof of the World
Chapter 2, "'Because It's There'"

Number the events in order from 1 to 5.

3 George Mallory and Andrew Irvine climbed to 26,800 feet.

1 In 1922 a team of British climbers tried to climb Mount Everest.

4 Noel Odell saw two small dots near the top of Everest.

2 Mallory returned with another British team to try to climb Mount Everest.

5 A snowstorm came, hiding Mallory and Irvine from view.

Mark each statement *T* for true or *F* for false.

T 1. The British paid Sherpas to be their guides.

F 2. The first people to die on Everest were two British climbers.

T 3. When asked why he wanted to climb Everest, Mallory said, "Because it's there!"

F 4. Odell found the bodies of Mallory and Irvine.

F 5. The bodies of Mallory and Irvine were discovered at the same time.

Read the question, and write your answer.

Why is it uncertain if Mallory and Irvine were the first climbers to reach the top of Mount Everest? **Ideas: They may have reached the summit of Everest during the snowstorm when Odell couldn't see them; Mallory's fatal fall may have occurred on his way back down.**

Discovery • Book 3   39

The Roof of the World

Chapter Quiz

Name _____ Date _____

The Roof of the World
Chapter 3, "Going Up"

Mark each statement *T* for true or *F* for false.

F 1. Edmund Hillary was born in Australia in 1919.

F 2. Hillary took care of sheep to train for climbing.

T 3. In 1951 a British team invited Hillary to join them to try to climb Everest.

T 4. One man on Hillary's team was a Sherpa named Tenzing Norgay.

F 5. The team had ten climbers and 20 Sherpa guides.

F 6. The team hiked 20 miles to get to the first camp on Everest.

F 7. The team had maps to help guide them through the Khumbu Icefall.

T 8. The Khumbu Icefall is made of big blocks of ice.

T 9. Norgay saved Hillary's life when Hillary started to fall into a crevasse.

F 10. The team made it from the Khumbu Icefall to the beginning of the Death Zone in about a week.

Read the question, and write your answer.

Why do climbers say Camp 8 is the beginning of the Death Zone? **Camp 8 is at 25,000 feet. At 25,000 feet, there is little oxygen in the air for people to breathe.**

40   Discovery • Book 3

The Roof of the World

---

46   Discovery • Book 3

Answer Key

Chapter Quiz

Name _____ Date _____

The Roof of the World
Chapter 4, "The Push to the Top"

Number the events in order from 1 to 5.

__2__ On May 28, Hillary and Norgay started out as the second summit team.

__5__ At night the wind almost tossed Hillary and Norgay off the mountain.

__3__ At 27,900 feet, Hillary and Norgay stopped to camp.

__4__ Hillary and Norgay melted snow to make hot drinks and ate crackers.

__1__ The first summit team had to turn back because their oxygen had run too low.

Number the events in order from 6 to 10.

__8__ Hillary and Norgay started up to the summit at six thirty in the morning.

__10__ Hillary and Norgay made it to the top of Mount Everest.

__6__ Hillary and Norgay got up at four o'clock in the morning on May 29.

__9__ Hillary spotted a crack in the steep wall of rock.

__7__ Hillary had to "cook" his boots to thaw them enough to get them on.

Read the question, and write your answer.

How long did Hillary and Norgay remain on the summit? Why didn't they stay longer on the top of the mountain? **They spent only 15 minutes on the summit. To stay longer would have been dangerous because their oxygen was running low.**

Discovery • Book 3   41

The Roof of the World

Chapter Quiz

Name _____ Date _____

The Roof of the World
Chapter 5, "Everest's Two Heroes"

Fill in the bubble beside the answer for each question.

1. Why did Norgay and Hillary look gloomy as they neared camp?
   - Ⓐ They had failed to reach the summit.
   - ● They were too tired to smile.
   - Ⓒ They thought their oxygen would run out before they made it safely down.

2. What did Queen Elizabeth II do for Hillary and Norgay?
   - ● She gave Norgay a medal and made Hillary a knight.
   - Ⓑ She gave them money to give to the Sherpa people.
   - Ⓒ She had newspaper photos of the two climbers taken and published.

3. Why does Hillary care deeply for the Sherpa people?
   - Ⓐ They are poor and need his help.
   - Ⓑ He admires their culture and traditional way of life.
   - ● He would most likely not have made it to the top of Everest without the help of Norgay and other Sherpas.

4. How has Hillary helped the Sherpa people?
   - Ⓐ He has encouraged banks to lend them money.
   - ● He has raised money to build schools and hospitals in Sherpa towns.
   - Ⓒ He has taught many Sherpas how to climb Mount Everest.

Read the question, and write your answer.

Why do you think Hillary and Norgay are considered heroes?
Ideas: They worked together and were the first to accomplish an amazing and very dangerous thing; they reached the highest spot of the world.

42   Discovery • Book 3

The Roof of the World

Chapter Quiz

Name _____ Date _____

The Roof of the World
Chapter 6, "Mount Everest Today"

Mark each statement T for true or F for false.

__F__ 1. In 1960 Hillary's son Peter climbed Mount Everest.

__T__ 2. More than 2,000 people have climbed to the top of Everest since 1953.

__F__ 3. Hillary thinks it is good that so many people are climbing Everest today.

__T__ 4. Climbers have left tents, oxygen tanks, ropes, and other trash on the mountain.

__T__ 5. Nepal is making new rules to help keep Everest clean.

__T__ 6. Climbers must now carry out all their trash and gear when they leave the mountain.

__T__ 7. Nepal made the area around Everest into a national park.

__F__ 8. Climbers can still cut down trees to use for cooking fires.

__T__ 9. It is dangerous for climbers to remain high on the mountain for too long.

__T__ 10. Many people still want to climb Mount Everest "because it's there."

Read the question, and write your answer.

Why won't Nepal cut back on the number of people it lets climb Everest each year? **Climbers pay Nepal a lot of money in order to get permission to climb; the country needs the money.**

Discovery • Book 3   43

The Roof of the World

Thinking and Writing

Name _____ Date _____

The Roof of the World
Think About It

Write about or give an oral presentation for each question.

1. Mallory claimed he wanted to climb Mount Everest "because it's there." What are some other reasons people climb mountains?
   Ideas: fastest or safest way to get to the other side; to get a good view of the countryside below; as a sport

2. Why do you think climbers going up Mount Everest go in teams?
   Ideas: to help carry equipment; to help lift each other up and down; for safety

3. If Nepal decides to limit the number of people who climb Mount Everest, how should the country do it? **Ideas: charge more for permits; institute a lottery for permits**

4. Would you ever climb a mountain? Why or why not? _____
   Answers will vary.

Write About It

Choose one of the questions below. Write your answer on a sheet of paper.

1. Imagine that you are Odell watching Mallory and Irvine on their way up to the summit and then seeing them disappear behind the clouds. Write a description of the climbing scene and explain how you feel.

2. Write a newspaper article for *The London Times* about Hillary and Norgay's successful climb to the summit of Mount Everest.

3. Write an informational article about the importance and accomplishments of the Sherpa guides on Everest.

4. Complete the Main Idea/Details Chart for this book.

44   Discovery • Book 3

The Roof of the World

Discovery • Book 3   47

Building Background

Name _____ Date _____

Stonehenge: A Special Place
What You Know

Write answers to these questions.

1. How do people mark the passage of time? _____
   _____

2. How do you think early people moved large, heavy objects?
   _____

3. Where is Stonehenge? Use an atlas or world map to help you locate it.
   _____

4. What are some of the monuments or tourist attractions in your area?
   _____
   _____

Word Meanings
Definitions

Look for these words as you read your chapter book. When you find one of these words, write its definition.

avenue: _____

bury: _____

grave: _____

middle: _____

sandstone: _____

temple: _____

48   Discovery • Book 4

Word Lists

Stonehenge: A Special Place

Unfamiliar Words	Word Meanings	Proper Nouns	
circle heavy half special place halfway sure	avenue middle	Stonehenge England Avon River	Chapter 1
break worship	temple grave		Chapter 2
bluestones			Chapter 3
stronger grease pairs modern	sandstone		Chapter 4
mounds dead dance	bury		Chapter 5
		Nebraska	Chapter 6

Discovery • Book 4

Chapter Quiz

Name _____ Date _____

Stonehenge: A Special Place
Chapter 1, "What Is Stonehenge?"

Mark each statement *T* for true or *F* for false.

_____ 1. Stonehenge is a square of stones located in England.

_____ 2. The stones are very old.

_____ 3. All of the original stones used at Stonehenge are still in place.

_____ 4. Almost all of the stones have pictures carved on them.

_____ 5. The people who made Stonehenge used wagons to move the stones.

_____ 6. Stonehenge has two doorways.

_____ 7. There is a path to the Avon River called the "Avenue."

_____ 8. The Heel Stone marks the spot where the sun comes up on the shortest day of the year.

_____ 9. Summer begins on the longest day of the year.

_____ 10. Winter begins on the shortest day of the year.

Read the question, and write your answer.

Why do you think ancient peoples carved pictures on some of the stones at Stonehenge? _____

_____

_____

Chapter Quiz

Name _____ Date _____

Stonehenge: A Special Place
Chapter 2, "The First People"

Fill in the bubble beside the answer for each question.

1. The people who made Stonehenge used tools made from
   - Ⓐ rocks.
   - Ⓑ wood.
   - Ⓒ animal bones.

2. Where does one Stonehenge doorway face?
   - Ⓐ where the sun comes up at the beginning of summer
   - Ⓑ where the Avon River begins to flow
   - Ⓒ where the sun comes up at the end of summer

3. Why did people chop down the trees at Stonehenge?
   - Ⓐ to fill in the earthen pits
   - Ⓑ to make poles
   - Ⓒ to clear the land so the stones could be placed

4. Where did the people who first made Stonehenge live?
   - Ⓐ at Stonehenge
   - Ⓑ in a nearby forest
   - Ⓒ on farms far away

Read the question, and write your answer.

Why might ancient peoples have been interested in marking the seasons?

_____

_____

Discovery • Book 4

Chapter Quiz

Name _____ Date _____

Stonehenge: A Special Place
Chapter 3, "The Bluestones"

Number the events in order from 1 to 5.

___ People wanted to make Stonehenge look new again.

___ People placed the bluestones in the center of Stonehenge.

___ Stonehenge was empty for 1,000 years.

___ People traveled far away to collect bluestones.

___ New people arrived at Stonehenge.

Number the events in order from 6 to 10.

___ People dragged the bluestones to the sea.

___ Boatloads of bluestones went up the river.

___ People made a path from the Avon River to a Stonehenge doorway.

___ People placed the bluestones so that they cut the Stonehenge circle in half.

___ People put the bluestones on boats.

Read the question, and write your answer.

Why might this second group of people have wanted to split the Stonehenge circle in half? _____

_____

_____

Chapter Quiz

Name _____ Date _____

Stonehenge: A Special Place
Chapter 4, "Slabs of Sandstone"

Mark each statement *T* for true or *F* for false.

____ 1. After many years, the bluestones became covered in dirt.

____ 2. The new people who came to Stonehenge decided to tear it down.

____ 3. The new stones at Stonehenge were slabs of sandstone.

____ 4. Each sandstone slab weighed about 40 tons.

____ 5. No one knows for sure how the stone slabs were moved to Stonehenge.

____ 6. People used tools to shape the stones.

____ 7. The stones were linked by vines.

____ 8. People dug pits to hold the stone slabs in place.

____ 9. Modern people have never been able to imitate how these slabs may have been placed.

____ 10. People dug up the bluestones and put them in a shape of a *U*.

Read the question, and write your answer.

Why do you think so little is known about Stonehenge and the people who created it? _____

_____

_____

Discovery • Book 4   53

Chapter Quiz

Name _____ Date _____

Stonehenge: A Special Place
Chapter 5, "Why Was It Made?"

Fill in the bubble beside the answer for each question.

1. Stonehenge was made
   - Ⓐ thousands of years ago.
   - Ⓑ millions of years ago.
   - Ⓒ a few years ago.

2. Sometimes the sun shines just right on the
   - Ⓐ head stone.
   - Ⓑ tallest stone.
   - Ⓒ heel stone.

3. Stonehenge has
   - Ⓐ many trees around.
   - Ⓑ a big city around it.
   - Ⓒ many graves around it.

4. The small hills around Stonehenge are called
   - Ⓐ bumps.
   - Ⓑ mounds.
   - Ⓒ lumps.

Read the question, and write your answer.

What do you think Stonehenge was used for? Explain your answer.

_____
_____

Chapter Quiz

Name _____ Date _____

Stonehenge: A Special Place
Chapter 6, "Stonehenge Today"

Mark each statement *T* for true or *F* for false.

____ 1. People are allowed to visit Stonehenge today.

____ 2. Many tall stones are still there.

____ 3. All of the bluestones are missing.

____ 4. People must hike hundreds of miles to visit Stonehenge.

____ 5. People can no longer see the grave sites.

____ 6. On one day per year people are allowed to go into the circle.

____ 7. On that day, people with special permits can stay to watch the sun come up.

____ 8. One plan to save Stonehenge is to move the parking lots far away.

____ 9. One man in Washington made his own Stonehenge.

____ 10. In Nebraska there is a Stonehenge made from refrigerators.

Read the question, and write your answer.

If you had the opportunity to visit Stonehenge, would you go? Why or why not? _____

_____

_____

Discovery • Book 4   55

Thinking and Writing

Name _____ Date _____

Stonehenge: A Special Place
Think About It

Write about or give an oral presentation for each question.

1. Today people are still interested in studying Stonehenge. Which modern building might future people be interested in studying? Explain your answer. _____

2. How does Stonehenge compare with the calendars people use today?

3. What tools might ancient people have used to move Stonehenge's big stones into place? What tools might they have used to carve the stones?

4. Why did modern people try to imitate the building of Stonehenge?

Write About It

Choose one of the questions below. Write your answer on a sheet of paper.

1. Using the description of Stonehenge in Chapter 1, draw a diagram of the site and write a paragraph-long caption for it.

2. Modern people have made their own versions of Stonehenge from flat stones and cars. If you were going to make your own version of Stonehenge, what materials would you use and why?

3. Create a travel brochure for Stonehenge, focusing on its many mysteries.

4. Complete the Making Inferences Chart for this book.

Discovery • Book 4

Fluency Passages

Stonehenge: A Special Place

Chapter 2 *pages 6 and 7*

*The people had tools made from animal bones. They used antlers as	12
picks to break up the dirt. They used big, wide bones to move the dirt up	28
and away.	30
They made two doorways—one on each side of the circle. They put	43
one doorway where the sun comes up at the beginning of summer. They	56
put the other doorway* where the sun sets at the beginning of winter. How	70
did they know where to put the doorways? No one knows for sure.	83

Chapter 6 *page 26*

*Many people go to Stonehenge on the longest day of the year. On	13
that day they can go inside the circle. Thousands of people go to watch the	28
sun come up. Some people wait all night. In the morning, the sun shines on	43
top of a special pair of stones.	50
Stonehenge is very old. It is falling down. Some people* want to do	63
more to save Stonehenge. They plan to move the parking lots farther away.	76
People will then have to walk more than two miles from the parking lot to	91
Stonehenge.	92

- The target rate for **Discovery** is 60 wcpm. The asterisks (*) mark 60 words.
- Listen to the student read the passage. Count the number of words read in one minute and the number of errors.
- For the reading rate, subtract the number of errors from the total number of words read.
- Have students enter their scores on their **Fluency Graph.** See page 9.

Discovery • Book 4

Answer Key

Building Background

Name _____ Date _____

Stonehenge: A Special Place
What You Know
Write answers to these questions.

1. How do people mark the passage of time? **Ideas: calendars, clocks, watches**

2. How do you think early people moved large, heavy objects? **Ideas: by dragging, rolling, pushing**

3. Where is Stonehenge? Use an atlas or world map to help you locate it. **Stonehenge is about 90 miles west of London, about ten miles from Salisbury.**

4. What are some of the monuments or tourist attractions in your area? **Answers will vary.**

Word Meanings
Definitions
Look for these words as you read your chapter book. When you find one of these words, write its definition.

avenue: **a wide, main street**
bury: **to put a dead body into the earth, a tomb, or the sea**
grave: **a place in the ground where a dead body is buried**
middle: **the point or part that is in the center**
sandstone: **a type of rock formed from sand held together by lime and other substances**
temple: **a building for the worship of a god**

48   Discovery • Book 4

Stonehenge: A Special Place

Chapter Quiz

Name _____ Date _____

Stonehenge: A Special Place
Chapter 1, "What Is Stonehenge?"
Mark each statement *T* for true or *F* for false.

F 1. Stonehenge is a square of stones located in England.
T 2. The stones are very old.
F 3. All of the original stones used at Stonehenge are still in place.
F 4. Almost all of the stones have pictures carved on them.
F 5. The people who made Stonehenge used wagons to move the stones.
T 6. Stonehenge has two doorways.
T 7. There is a path to the Avon River called the "Avenue."
F 8. The Heel Stone marks the spot where the sun comes up on the shortest day of the year.
T 9. Summer begins on the longest day of the year.
T 10. Winter begins on the shortest day of the year.

Read the question, and write your answer.

Why do you think ancient peoples carved pictures on some of the stones at Stonehenge? **Ideas: to record history, beliefs, values**

50   Discovery • Book 4

Stonehenge: A Special Place

Chapter Quiz

Name _____ Date _____

Stonehenge: A Special Place
Chapter 2, "The First People"
Fill in the bubble beside the answer for each question.

1. The people who made Stonehenge used tools made from
   Ⓐ rocks.
   Ⓑ wood.
   ● animal bones.

2. Where does one Stonehenge doorway face?
   ● where the sun comes up at the beginning of summer
   Ⓑ where the Avon River begins to flow
   Ⓒ where the sun comes up at the end of summer

3. Why did people chop down the trees at Stonehenge?
   Ⓐ to fill in the earthen pits
   ● to make poles
   Ⓒ to clear the land so the stones could be placed

4. Where did the people who first made Stonehenge live?
   Ⓐ at Stonehenge
   Ⓑ in a nearby forest
   ● on farms far away

Read the question, and write your answer.

Why might ancient peoples have been interested in marking the seasons? **Idea: Marking the seasons would help farmers know when to plant and harvest their crops.**

Discovery • Book 4   51

Stonehenge: A Special Place

Chapter Quiz

Name _____ Date _____

Stonehenge: A Special Place
Chapter 3, "The Bluestones"
Number the events in order from 1 to 5.

3 People wanted to make Stonehenge look new again.
5 People placed the bluestones in the center of Stonehenge.
1 Stonehenge was empty for 1,000 years.
4 People traveled far away to collect bluestones.
2 New people arrived at Stonehenge.

Number the events in order from 6 to 10.

6 People dragged the bluestones to the sea.
8 Boatloads of bluestones went up the river.
9 People made a path from the Avon River to a Stonehenge doorway.
10 People placed the bluestones so that they cut the Stonehenge circle in half.
7 People put the bluestones on boats.

Read the question, and write your answer.

Why might this second group of people have wanted to split the Stonehenge circle in half? **Accept reasonable responses.**

52   Discovery • Book 4

Stonehenge: A Special Place

---

58   Discovery • Book 4

Answer Key

Chapter Quiz

Name _____ Date _____

Stonehenge: A Special Place
Chapter 4, "Slabs of Sandstone"

Mark each statement *T* for true or *F* for false.

__T__ 1. After many years, the bluestones became covered in dirt.
__F__ 2. The new people who came to Stonehenge decided to tear it down.
__T__ 3. The new stones at Stonehenge were slabs of sandstone.
__T__ 4. Each sandstone slab weighed about 40 tons.
__T__ 5. No one knows for sure how the stone slabs were moved to Stonehenge.
__T__ 6. People used tools to shape the stones.
__F__ 7. The stones were linked by vines.
__T__ 8. People dug pits to hold the stone slabs in place.
__F__ 9. Modern people have never been able to imitate how these slabs may have been placed.
__T__ 10. People dug up the bluestones and put them in a shape of a *U*.

Read the question, and write your answer.

Why do you think so little is known about Stonehenge and the people who created it? **Ideas: happened thousands of years ago; no written records; little physical evidence**

Discovery • Book 4   53

Stonehenge: A Special Place

Chapter Quiz

Name _____ Date _____

Stonehenge: A Special Place
Chapter 5, "Why Was It Made?"

Fill in the bubble beside the answer for each question.

1. Stonehenge was made
   ● thousands of years ago.
   Ⓑ millions of years ago.
   Ⓒ a few years ago.

2. Sometimes the sun shines just right on the
   Ⓐ head stone.
   Ⓑ tallest stone.
   ● heel stone.

3. Stonehenge has
   Ⓐ many trees around.
   Ⓑ a big city around it.
   ● many graves around it.

4. The small hills around Stonehenge are called
   Ⓐ bumps.
   ● mounds.
   Ⓒ lumps.

Read the question, and write your answer.

What do you think Stonehenge was used for? Explain your answer.
Accept reasonable responses.

54   Discovery • Book 4

Stonehenge: A Special Place

Chapter Quiz

Name _____ Date _____

Stonehenge: A Special Place
Chapter 6, "Stonehenge Today"

Mark each statement *T* for true or *F* for false.

__T__ 1. People are allowed to visit Stonehenge today.
__T__ 2. Many tall stones are still there.
__F__ 3. All of the bluestones are missing.
__F__ 4. People must hike hundreds of miles to visit Stonehenge.
__F__ 5. People can no longer see the grave sites.
__T__ 6. On one day per year people are allowed to go into the circle.
__F__ 7. On that day, people with special permits can stay to watch the sun come up.
__T__ 8. One plan to save Stonehenge is to move the parking lots far away.
__T__ 9. One man in Washington made his own Stonehenge.
__F__ 10. In Nebraska there is a Stonehenge made from refrigerators.

Read the question, and write your answer.

If you had the opportunity to visit Stonehenge, would you go? Why or why not? **Accept reasonable responses.**

Discovery • Book 4   55

Stonehenge: A Special Place

Thinking and Writing

Name _____ Date _____

Stonehenge: A Special Place
Think About It

Write about or give an oral presentation for each question.

1. Today people are still interested in studying Stonehenge. Which modern building might future people be interested in studying? Explain your answer. **Accept reasonable responses.**

2. How does Stonehenge compare with the calendars people use today? **Ideas: Modern calendars and Stonehenge both mark the seasons and include notations for the first days of summer and winter.**

3. What tools might ancient people have used to move Stonehenge's big stones into place? What tools might they have used to carve the stones? **Ideas: sleds, ramps, boats, ropes, animals; tools made of wood, stone, bone, or shells**

4. Why did modern people try to imitate the building of Stonehenge? **Ideas: admiration; curiosity; to learn about ancient history and culture**

Write About It

Choose one of the questions below. Write your answer on a sheet of paper.

1. Using the description of Stonehenge in Chapter 1, draw a diagram of the site and write a paragraph-long caption for it.

2. Modern people have made their own versions of Stonehenge from flat stones and cars. If you were going to make your own version of Stonehenge, what materials would you use and why?

3. Create a travel brochure for Stonehenge, focusing on its many mysteries.

4. Complete the Making Inferences Chart for this book.

56   Discovery • Book 4

Stonehenge: A Special Place

Discovery • Book 4   59

Building Background

Name _____ Date _____

Shipwrecks and Their Secrets
What You Know

Write answers to these questions.

1. What are some of the causes of shipwrecks? _____
   _____

2. What kinds of things do you think early explorers took with them when they sailed? _____
   _____

3. If you were traveling on a boat in a heavy fog or terrible storm, what would you do to try to protect yourself? _____
   _____

4. Begin the What I Know/What I Learned Chart for this book.

Word Meanings
Synonyms and Antonyms

Look for these words as you read your chapter book. When you find a word, write a synonym or antonym for the word.

Synonyms

apart: _____

jewelry: _____

robot: _____

sunken: _____

Antonyms

sure: _____

valuable: _____

60   Discovery • Book 5

Word Lists

Shipwrecks and Their Secrets

Unfamiliar Words	Word Meanings	Proper Nouns	
changes harmonicas scientists seawater secrets shipwrecks wartime	apart		Chapter 1
captain learn scratched	jewelry	Uluburun [oo-LYOO- boo-run]	Chapter 2
passengers	sunken	California Central America New York Panama Atlantic Ocean	Chapter 3
great pressure radar shocked supposed torpedo unsinkable warship	sure	Andrea Doria Canada Empress of Ireland England Europe Germany Lusitania World War I	Chapter 4
artifacts breath coins reasons scuba vacuum	valuable		Chapter 5
bubbles sonar studying submersibles tech	robot	Nemo	Chapter 6

Discovery • Book 5

Chapter Quiz

Name _____ Date _____

Shipwrecks and Their Secrets
Chapter 1, "A Watery Grave"

Fill in the bubble beside the answer for each question.

1. Which of the following might cause a ship to sink?
    - Ⓐ weather
    - Ⓑ traffic
    - Ⓒ birds

2. What is another thing that might cause a ship to sink?
    - Ⓐ sea animals
    - Ⓑ bridges
    - Ⓒ an attack from another ship

3. Seawater causes some items, such as paper or cloth, to
    - Ⓐ float.
    - Ⓑ rot.
    - Ⓒ keep their form.

4. Seawater and small animals cause other items to
    - Ⓐ rot and disappear.
    - Ⓑ change form.
    - Ⓒ keep their form.

Read the question, and write your answer.

Why do scientists study shipwrecks? _____
_____
_____

Chapter Quiz

Name _____ Date _____

Shipwrecks and Their Secrets
Chapter 2, "The First Shipwrecks"

Mark each statement *T* for true or *F* for false.

___ 1. In 1982 divers found a shipwreck that was 3,300 years old.

___ 2. The wreck was located near Uluburun, Turkey.

___ 3. Divers did not find any gold or jewelry on board.

___ 4. Divers found a paper book on board.

___ 5. The book was probably used as the captain's personal journal.

___ 6. The sea near Uluburun was once busy with trade ships.

___ 7. Studying wrecks in this area helps scientists learn about trade goods from long ago.

___ 8. Studying wrecks in this area also helps scientists learn about ancient trade routes.

___ 9. There are over 200 shipwrecks near Uluburun.

___ 10. Some of the ships sank over 2,000 years ago.

Read the question, and write your answer.

Why do scientists want to learn about trade during historic times?

_____

_____

_____

Discovery • Book 5

Chapter Quiz

Name _____ Date _____

Shipwrecks and Their Secrets
Chapter 3, "Sunken Gold"

Number the events in order from 1 to 5.

____ A big storm hit.

____ The ship sank.

____ Sailors put up the sails, but the wind tore them.

____ Waves crashing over the deck put out the fires needed to make steam.

____ The *Central America* left Panama and headed toward New York.

Mark each statement *T* for true or *F* for false.

____ 1. The *Central America* was a trade ship.

____ 2. The *Central America* was a small ship.

____ 3. The *Central America* survived for more than two days before sinking.

____ 4. The *Central America* sank with millions of dollars of gold.

____ 5. Over 300 years passed before the wreck was discovered.

Read the question, and write your answer.

Why was the *Central America* carrying so much treasure on it?

_____
_____
_____

64   Discovery • Book 5

Chapter Quiz

Name _____ Date _____

Shipwrecks and Their Secrets
Chapter 4, "Unsinkable?"

Fill in the bubble beside the answer for each question.

1. What caused the *Empress of Ireland* to sink?
   - Ⓐ It was destroyed during a storm.
   - Ⓑ Another ship crashed into it in the fog.
   - Ⓒ It was hit while it was docked on a riverbank.

2. Why did the *Empress of Ireland* sink so quickly?
   - Ⓐ People had left windows and doors open, allowing the ship to fill with water.
   - Ⓑ The ship broke in half, and both parts went down.
   - Ⓒ Three big holes formed in the sides of the ship.

3. What caused the *Lusitania* to sink?
   - Ⓐ It crashed into another ship.
   - Ⓑ It was caught in a terrible storm.
   - Ⓒ It was attacked by a German boat.

4. The *Andrea Doria* had a new tool called
   - Ⓐ sonar.
   - Ⓑ radar.
   - Ⓒ lunar.

Read the question, and write your answer.

Despite improvements in technology, three ships—the *Empress of Ireland,* the *Lusitania,* and the *Andrea Doria*—sank. What common element caused the ships to sink? _____

_____

_____

Discovery • Book 5

Chapter Quiz

Name _____ Date _____

Shipwrecks and Their Secrets
Chapter 5, "Getting to the Bottom"

Mark each statement *T* for true or *F* for false.

___ 1. People buy shipwrecks and pay divers to recover the goods from them.

___ 2. Some people steal artifacts from shipwrecks they do not own.

___ 3. Early divers used scuba gear.

___ 4. Today, even the best divers can stay under water for only a few minutes.

___ 5. Divers and scientists work together to photograph and retrieve artifacts.

Number the events in order from 1 to 5.

___ Divers hooked ropes to the bolts.

___ People view a display of the *Mary Rose* today in England.

___ The *Mary Rose* sank in 1545.

___ Divers placed bolts along the wreck.

___ Divers pulled the ship from the water.

Read the question, and write your answer.

What is the relationship between scientists and looters?

_____

_____

_____

Chapter Quiz

Name _____ Date _____

Shipwrecks and Their Secrets
Chapter 6, "Wreck Tech"

Fill in the bubble beside the answer for each question.

1. Divers must be careful to
   - Ⓐ stay in shallow water.
   - Ⓑ stay under water for more than 20 minutes.
   - Ⓒ swim slowly to the surface.

2. What do scientists use to study deep wrecks?
   - Ⓐ submersibles
   - Ⓑ robots
   - Ⓒ both A and B

3. How do scientists find missing wrecks?
   - Ⓐ sonar
   - Ⓑ radar
   - Ⓒ satellites

4. How did *Nemo* recover gold from the *Central America*?
   - Ⓐ slime
   - Ⓑ cages
   - Ⓒ nets

Read the question, and write your answer.

Do you agree that developing tools to explore shipwrecks is worth the cost? Explain your answer. _____

_____

_____

Discovery • Book 5

Thinking and Writing

Name _____ Date _____

Shipwrecks and Their Secrets
Think About It

Write about or give an oral presentation for each question.

1. What is the most dangerous situation a ship might face? Explain your answer. _____

2. If treasure and gold were not contained in shipwrecks, would people be as interested in exploring them? Explain your answer.
_____

3. Why do people want to think that ships are unsinkable? _____
_____

4. Should shipwrecks be bought and sold among specific owners, or should they belong to everyone? Explain your answer.
_____
_____

Write About It

Choose one of the questions below. Write your answer on a sheet of paper.

1. Scientists think some of the items found at the Uluburun wreck may have been gifts for a king. If you had to gather modern gifts for an ocean journey to visit the king or queen of another country, what would you give him or her and why? Create a gift list with an explanation for each item.

2. Write a brief newspaper article telling about the sinking of the *Lusitania*.

3. Complete the What I Know/What I Learned Chart for this book.

Fluency Passages

Shipwrecks and Their Secrets

Chapter 1 *page 1*

*The sea can be very hard on ships. High waves can fill a ship with	15
water. Fog can make a ship crash into rocks, ice, or another ship. In	29
wartime, other ships may attack. Any of these things can sink a ship.	42
Many shipwrecks are at the bottom of the sea. Some have been there	55
for many years. The way* they look changes over time.	65
The seawater makes some things fall apart. Most cloth and paper rot	77
away. But the seawater and the lack of air help keep other things from	91
rotting.	92

Chapter 6 *page 25*

*Divers can't dive much deeper than 100 feet. But many wrecks are	12
much deeper than that. To study deep wrecks, scientists sometimes use	23
submersibles. These are small ships that can go deep under water.	34
Submersibles can go up to 15,000 feet below the surface. That is very	47
deep. It can take hours for them to get to a wreck that* deep. The scientists	63
can't get out of the submersible to look around when they get to a	77
shipwreck. But they can look out of windows and take pictures.	88

- The target rate for **Discovery** is 60 wcpm. The asterisks (*) mark 60 words.

- Listen to the student read the passage. Count the number of words read in one minute and the number of errors.

- For the reading rate, subtract the number of errors from the total number of words read.

- Have students enter their scores on their **Fluency Graph.** See page 9.

Answer Key

Building Background

Name _____ Date _____

Shipwrecks and Their Secrets
What You Know
Write answers to these questions.

1. What are some of the causes of shipwrecks? **Ideas: ships hit other ships or large objects; go down in storms; run aground**

2. What kinds of things do you think early explorers took with them when they sailed? **Ideas: different kinds of supplies, animals, valuables, trade goods**

3. If you were traveling on a boat in a heavy fog or terrible storm, what would you do to try to protect yourself? **Accept reasonable responses.**

4. Begin the What I Know/What I Learned Chart for this book.

Word Meanings
Synonyms and Antonyms
Look for these words as you read your chapter book. When you find a word, write a synonym or antonym for the word.

Synonyms
- apart: **to pieces, to bits**
- jewelry: **gems, trinkets**
- robot: **gadget, computer**
- sunken: **below ground level, at a lower level**

Antonyms
- sure: **doubtful, uncertain**
- valuable: **cheap, worthless**

60 — Discovery • Book 5
Shipwrecks and Their Secrets

Chapter Quiz

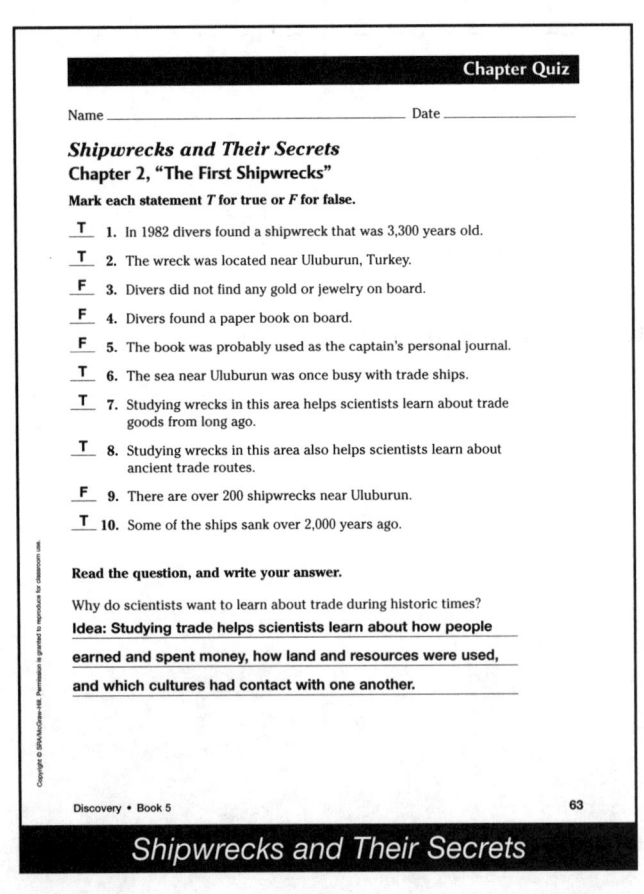

Name _____ Date _____

Shipwrecks and Their Secrets
Chapter 1, "A Watery Grave"
Fill in the bubble beside the answer for each question.

1. Which of the following might cause a ship to sink?
   - ● weather
   - Ⓑ traffic
   - Ⓒ birds

2. What is another thing that might cause a ship to sink?
   - Ⓐ sea animals
   - Ⓑ bridges
   - ● an attack from another ship

3. Seawater causes some items, such as paper or cloth, to
   - Ⓐ float.
   - ● rot.
   - Ⓒ keep their form.

4. Seawater and small animals cause other items to
   - Ⓐ rot and disappear.
   - Ⓑ change form.
   - ● keep their form.

Read the question, and write your answer.
Why do scientists study shipwrecks? **Ideas: to learn about past peoples and cultures; to recover valuable artifacts**

62 — Discovery • Book 5
Shipwrecks and Their Secrets

Chapter Quiz

Name _____ Date _____

Shipwrecks and Their Secrets
Chapter 2, "The First Shipwrecks"
Mark each statement *T* for true or *F* for false.

- **T** 1. In 1982 divers found a shipwreck that was 3,300 years old.
- **T** 2. The wreck was located near Uluburun, Turkey.
- **F** 3. Divers did not find any gold or jewelry on board.
- **F** 4. Divers found a paper book on board.
- **F** 5. The book was probably used as the captain's personal journal.
- **T** 6. The sea near Uluburun was once busy with trade ships.
- **T** 7. Studying wrecks in this area helps scientists learn about trade goods from long ago.
- **T** 8. Studying wrecks in this area also helps scientists learn about ancient trade routes.
- **F** 9. There are over 200 shipwrecks near Uluburun.
- **T** 10. Some of the ships sank over 2,000 years ago.

Read the question, and write your answer.
Why do scientists want to learn about trade during historic times?
Idea: Studying trade helps scientists learn about how people earned and spent money, how land and resources were used, and which cultures had contact with one another.

Discovery • Book 5 — 63
Shipwrecks and Their Secrets

Chapter Quiz

Name _____ Date _____

Shipwrecks and Their Secrets
Chapter 3, "Sunken Gold"
Number the events in order from 1 to 5.

- **2** A big storm hit.
- **5** The ship sank.
- **4** Sailors put up the sails, but the wind tore them.
- **3** Waves crashing over the deck put out the fires needed to make steam.
- **1** The *Central America* left Panama and headed toward New York.

Mark each statement *T* for true or *F* for false.

- **F** 1. The *Central America* was a trade ship.
- **F** 2. The *Central America* was a small ship.
- **T** 3. The *Central America* survived for more than two days before sinking.
- **T** 4. The *Central America* sank with millions of dollars of gold.
- **F** 5. Over 300 years passed before the wreck was discovered.

Read the question, and write your answer.
Why was the *Central America* carrying so much treasure on it?
It was carrying people who had gotten rich as a result of the California gold rush, and they had their gold with them.

64 — Discovery • Book 5
Shipwrecks and Their Secrets

---

70 — Discovery • Book 5

Answer Key

Chapter Quiz

Name _____ Date _____

Shipwrecks and Their Secrets
Chapter 4, "Unsinkable?"

Fill in the bubble beside the answer for each question.

1. What caused the *Empress of Ireland* to sink?
   - Ⓐ It was destroyed during a storm.
   - ● Another ship crashed into it in the fog.
   - Ⓒ It was hit while it was docked on a riverbank.

2. Why did the *Empress of Ireland* sink so quickly?
   - ● People had left windows and doors open, allowing the ship to fill with water.
   - Ⓑ The ship broke in half, and both parts went down.
   - Ⓒ Three big holes formed in the sides of the ship.

3. What caused the *Lusitania* to sink?
   - Ⓐ It crashed into another ship.
   - Ⓑ It was caught in a terrible storm.
   - ● It was attacked by a German boat.

4. The *Andrea Doria* had a new tool called
   - Ⓐ sonar.
   - ● radar.
   - Ⓒ lunar.

Read the question, and write your answer.

Despite improvements in technology, three ships—the *Empress of Ireland*, the *Lusitania*, and the *Andrea Doria*—sank. What common element caused the ships to sink? **Humans contributed to the sinking of all three ships.**

Discovery • Book 5   65

Shipwrecks and Their Secrets

Chapter Quiz

Name _____ Date _____

Shipwrecks and Their Secrets
Chapter 5, "Getting to the Bottom"

Mark each statement *T* for true or *F* for false.

- **T** 1. People buy shipwrecks and pay divers to recover the goods from them.
- **T** 2. Some people steal artifacts from shipwrecks they do not own.
- **F** 3. Early divers used scuba gear.
- **F** 4. Today, even the best divers can stay under water for only a few minutes.
- **T** 5. Divers and scientists work together to photograph and retrieve artifacts.

Number the events in order from 1 to 5.

- **3** Divers hooked ropes to the bolts.
- **5** People view a display of the *Mary Rose* today in England.
- **1** The *Mary Rose* sank in 1545.
- **2** Divers placed bolts along the wreck.
- **4** Divers pulled the ship from the water.

Read the question, and write your answer.

What is the relationship between scientists and looters? **Scientists want shipwrecks to remain as they are so the ships and artifacts can be studied to learn about the past. Looters steal artifacts from ships to make money. Scientists want looters stopped because the missing artifacts make it more difficult for scientists to do their work.**

66   Discovery • Book 5

Shipwrecks and Their Secrets

Chapter Quiz

Name _____ Date _____

Shipwrecks and Their Secrets
Chapter 6, "Wreck Tech"

Fill in the bubble beside the answer for each question.

1. Divers must be careful to
   - Ⓐ stay in shallow water.
   - Ⓑ stay under water for more than 20 minutes.
   - ● swim slowly to the surface.

2. What do scientists use to study deep wrecks?
   - Ⓐ submersibles
   - Ⓑ robots
   - ● both A and B

3. How do scientists find missing wrecks?
   - ● sonar
   - Ⓑ radar
   - Ⓒ satellites

4. How did *Nemo* recover gold from the *Central America*?
   - ● slime
   - Ⓑ cages
   - Ⓒ nets

Read the question, and write your answer.

Do you agree that developing tools to explore shipwrecks is worth the cost? Explain your answer. **Ideas: Studying the past provides insights into present and future choices; there are more important programs on which to spend money.**

Discovery • Book 5   67

Shipwrecks and Their Secrets

Thinking and Writing

Name _____ Date _____

Shipwrecks and Their Secrets
Think About It

Write about or give an oral presentation for each question.

1. What is the most dangerous situation a ship might face? Explain your answer. **Accept reasonable responses.**

2. If treasure and gold were not contained in shipwrecks, would people be as interested in exploring them? Explain your answer.
   Ideas: Many people are motivated by money. The historic gains alone would probably not motivate many explorers.

3. Why do people want to think that ships are unsinkable? **People want to feel safe or want to think they have gained power over nature.**

4. Should shipwrecks be bought and sold among specific owners, or should they belong to everyone? Explain your answer.
   Ideas: People do not own the ocean, so they cannot own things on the ocean floor; information to be gained by exploring these wrecks can only be preserved through ownership.

Write About It

Choose one of the questions below. Write your answer on a sheet of paper.

1. Scientists think some of the items found at the Uluburun wreck may have been gifts for a king. If you had to gather modern gifts for an ocean journey to visit the king or queen of another country, what would you give him or her and why? Create a gift list with an explanation for each item.

2. Write a brief newspaper article telling about the sinking of the *Lusitania*.

3. Complete the What I Know/What I Learned Chart for this book.

68   Discovery • Book 5

Shipwrecks and Their Secrets

Discovery • Book 5   71

Building Background

Name _____ Date _____

Migrating Creatures Big and Small
What You Know

Write answers to these questions.

1. Think about a time you have seen a butterfly. What did it look like? What time of year was it? _____

2. Research bison at Yellowstone National Park. Why was a safe place for bison created at Yellowstone? About how many bison are in Yellowstone? _____
_____

3. Give a short definition of *migration*. _____
_____

Word Meanings
Definitions

Look for these words as you read your chapter book. When you find a word, draw a line to connect the word with the correct definition.

beach	a leaping insect that has two pairs of wings and strong hind legs
bison	a diving bird that looks like a duck but has a pointed bill and a weird cry
butterfly	a smooth, sloping stretch of sand and pebbles at the edge of a sea, lake, or other body of water
grasshopper	the sweet liquid in many flowers, made into honey by bees
loon	an insect with a slender body and four broad wings, usually brightly colored
nectar	a wild animal that has a shaggy mane, short, curved horns, and a humped back

72   Discovery • Book 6

Word Lists

Migrating Creatures Big and Small

	Unfamiliar Words	Word Meanings	Proper Nouns	
	backwards creatures directions energy farther hover learn migrate northern perch place weight	nectar	Canada Gulf of Mexico United States	Chapter 1
	turtle	beach		Chapter 2
	catch hatch parents south young	loon		Chapter 3
	eastern enough fir monarch butterfly square tailwind volunteer	butterfly		Chapter 4
	elk roam rules safety	bison	Montana Yellowstone National Park Wyoming	Chapter 5
	different freshwater nature spawn trout	grasshopper		Chapter 6

Discovery • Book 6

73

Chapter Quiz

Name _____ Date _____

Migrating Creatures Big and Small
Introduction and Chapter 1, "The Hummingbird"

Mark each statement *T* for true or *F* for false.

_____ 1. For all animals, migration is a way to stay alive.

_____ 2. When an animal migrates, it moves from one place to another place far away.

_____ 3. Hummingbirds are about the same size as most birds.

_____ 4. Each year the hummingbird flies farther than every other bird.

_____ 5. There are over 300 kinds of hummingbirds.

_____ 6. When it first comes out of its egg, a hummingbird is the size of a bee.

_____ 7. Hummingbirds can fly in all directions except backwards.

_____ 8. Hummingbirds are sometimes called "flower kissers."

_____ 9. Hummingbirds migrate to Mexico in the summer.

_____ 10. Hummingbirds migrate to the northern United States and Canada in the winter.

Read the question, and write your answer.

How does migration help the hummingbird survive? _____

_____

_____

Chapter Quiz

Name _____ Date _____

Migrating Creatures Big and Small
Chapter 2, "Sea Turtles on the Run"

Fill in the bubble beside the answer for each question.

1. A mother sea turtle nests
   - Ⓐ in grasses close to the beach.
   - Ⓑ on the same beach she was born on.
   - Ⓒ away from bright lights.

2. The first 100 feet of the turtle's migration
   - Ⓐ is the hardest part of its trip.
   - Ⓑ is the safest part of its trip.
   - Ⓒ is the fastest part of its trip.

3. Only a few baby sea turtles
   - Ⓐ get lost.
   - Ⓑ get eaten.
   - Ⓒ make it to the sea.

4. Some people try to help the sea turtles
   - Ⓐ by tagging the male turtles.
   - Ⓑ by putting tags on one of their legs.
   - Ⓒ by making the beaches safe for the baby turtles.

Read the question, and write your answer.

Why do you think baby turtles start their trip at night? _____

_____

_____

Discovery • Book 6

Chapter Quiz

Name _____ Date _____

Migrating Creatures Big and Small
Chapter 3, "The Loon Family"

Mark each statement *T* for true or *F* for false.

_____ 1. The loon has black and white spots, a black head, and black eyes.

_____ 2. In the summer, the loon's home is in warmer places near the ocean.

_____ 3. Getting into the air is hard for the loon.

_____ 4. A good spot for a loon's nest is in trees near the shore.

_____ 5. The mother loon lays two eggs.

_____ 6. The loon parents fly south together for the winter.

_____ 7. The loon parents come back to the same nest in the spring.

_____ 8. The young loons leave with their parents in late fall.

_____ 9. Young loons won't go north again until they are three years old.

_____ 10. The loon has five major calls.

Read the question, and write your answer.

What are the meanings of the loon's calls? _____

_____

_____

Chapter Quiz

Name _____ Date _____

Migrating Creatures Big and Small
Chapter 4, "The Monarch Butterfly"

Fill in the bubble beside the answer for each question.

1. Monarch butterflies
   - Ⓐ lay their eggs only on milkweed plants.
   - Ⓑ are found in the western part of Canada and the United States.
   - Ⓒ fly all the way to Mexico in the spring.

2. The monarch travels
   - Ⓐ up to 2,000 miles each year.
   - Ⓑ farther than any bird.
   - Ⓒ farther than any other butterfly.

3. The Mexican fir tree
   - Ⓐ helps the butterflies lay their eggs in the fall.
   - Ⓑ is the monarch's best spot to land.
   - Ⓒ covers over 2,000 square miles of Mexico today.

4. Young monarchs
   - Ⓐ follow their parents to the same spot each year.
   - Ⓑ always go back to the same tree each year.
   - Ⓒ go to the same spot their parents were the spring before.

Read the question, and write your answer.

What is one thing you would like to learn about monarch butterflies?

_____

_____

_____

Discovery • Book 6

Chapter Quiz

Name _____ Date _____

Migrating Creatures Big and Small
Chapter 5, "Where Can the Bison Roam?"

Mark each statement *T* for true or *F* for false.

_____ 1. Bison are one of the biggest land animals.

_____ 2. Bison begin their migration at Yellowstone National Park.

_____ 3. Bison travel 200 miles each way.

_____ 4. Bison with tags can be tracked.

_____ 5. Boris was a bison whose tag fell off.

_____ 6. Because bison are big, migration is not hard.

_____ 7. The state of Montana has rules about where bison can go.

_____ 8. The rules help bison know where they can go.

_____ 9. Sometimes the bison at Yellowstone get too close to people.

_____ 10. Bison do not have a place to safely roam.

Read the question, and write your answer.

Why do you think the bison is one of the United States' most loved animals?

_____

_____

Chapter Quiz

Name _____ Date _____

Migrating Creatures Big and Small
Chapter 6, "Trout Making a Splash"

Fill in the bubble beside the answer for each question.

1. Trout that live in both freshwater and salt water
   - Ⓐ are the biggest trout.
   - Ⓑ are called "sea-run" trout.
   - Ⓒ lay their eggs in shallow parts of the ocean.

2. Trout migrate
   - Ⓐ using their sense of smell to guide them.
   - Ⓑ to the ocean to lay their eggs.
   - Ⓒ from coasts to deep parts of the ocean.

3. Trout lay their eggs
   - Ⓐ in the place where they were born.
   - Ⓑ in deep waters.
   - Ⓒ in warm waters.

4. What happens when trout run into a waterfall on their way?
   - Ⓐ They find a different way to go.
   - Ⓑ They know of ways that don't have waterfalls.
   - Ⓒ They keep leaping until they make it to the top of the waterfall.

Read the question, and write your answer.

Why do trout that live in the ocean have to migrate? _____

_____

Discovery • Book 6

Thinking and Writing

Name _____ Date _____

Migrating Creatures Big and Small
Think About It

Write about or give an oral presentation for each question.

1. Choose two animals from this book. Compare their migrations. How are they similar? How are they different? _____
   _____

2. Name ways that migration helps animals. _____
   _____
   _____

3. Name one way people cause problems for migrating animals.
   _____
   _____

4. What is one way tagging helps animals? _____
   _____
   _____
   _____

Write About It

Choose one of the questions below. Write your answer on a sheet of paper.

1. Pretend you work at Yellowstone National Park. What rules would you make to protect the bison?

2. If you could help tag one of the animals mentioned in this book, which one would it be? Give reasons for your answer.

3. Complete the Content Web for this book.

80   Discovery • Book 6

Fluency Passages

Migrating Creatures Big and Small

Chapter 2 *page 9*

*Sometimes the baby turtles see bright lights. They think the lights	11
are on the water. But the lights may be from a beach store or a fast-food	27
place. The turtles get lost. They don't know which way to go. If they head	42
for the lights, another animal could snap them up.	51
Only a few baby turtles make it to the* sea. They dive in and swim	66
fast. They keep swimming for 24 hours or more. They swim deep into the	80
sea to keep safe.	84

Chapter 6 *pages 24 and 25*

*Trout are fish that have pretty red, gold, green, and blue scales.	12
These scales have a slippery covering. This covering keeps the trout from	24
getting sick.	26
A trout eats smaller fish for food. But trout will also jump out of the	41
water for food. A grasshopper that has left the safety of land can be a	56
trout's meal in a* splash.	61
Most trout like cool freshwater. But some live in salt water too.	73
Trout that live in both freshwater and salt water are called "sea-run"	85
trout.	86

- The target rate for **Discovery** is 60 wcpm. The asterisks (*) mark 60 words.

- Listen to the student read the passage. Count the number of words read in one minute and the number of errors.

- For the reading rate, subtract the number of errors from the total number of words read.

- Have students enter their scores on their **Fluency Graph.** See page 9.

Discovery • Book 6

Answer Key

Building Background

Name _____ Date _____

Migrating Creatures Big and Small
What You Know
Write answers to these questions.

1. Think about a time you have seen a butterfly. What did it look like? What time of year was it? **Accept reasonable responses.**

2. Research bison at Yellowstone National Park. Why was a safe place for bison created at Yellowstone? About how many bison are in Yellowstone? **By the late 1800s, there were only about 1,000 bison left in the United States because hunters and poachers had killed so many. There are now over 3,000 bison in Yellowstone.**

3. Give a short definition of *migration*. **Migration is moving from one place to another place far away.**

Word Meanings
Definitions
Look for these words as you read your chapter book. When you find a word, draw a line to connect the word with the correct definition.

beach — a smooth, sloping stretch of sand and pebbles at the edge of a sea, lake, or other body of water
bison — a wild animal that has a shaggy mane, short, curved horns, and a humped back
butterfly — an insect with a slender body and four broad wings, usually brightly colored
grasshopper — a leaping insect that has two pairs of wings and strong hind legs
loon — a diving bird that looks like a duck but has a pointed bill and a weird cry
nectar — the sweet liquid in many flowers, made into honey by bees

72 Discovery • Book 6

Migrating Creatures Big and Small

Chapter Quiz

Name _____ Date _____

Migrating Creatures Big and Small
Introduction and Chapter 1, "The Hummingbird"
Mark each statement *T* for true or *F* for false.

F 1. For all animals, migration is a way to stay alive.
T 2. When an animal migrates, it moves from one place to another place far away.
F 3. Hummingbirds are about the same size as most birds.
F 4. Each year the hummingbird flies farther than every other bird.
T 5. There are over 300 kinds of hummingbirds.
T 6. When it first comes out of its egg, a hummingbird is the size of a bee.
F 7. Hummingbirds can fly in all directions except backwards.
T 8. Hummingbirds are sometimes called "flower kissers."
F 9. Hummingbirds migrate to Mexico in the summer.
F 10. Hummingbirds migrate to the northern United States and Canada in the winter.

Read the question, and write your answer.

How does migration help the hummingbird survive? **The hummingbird migrates to warmer climates in winter so the winter cold does not freeze them.**

74 Discovery • Book 6

Migrating Creatures Big and Small

Chapter Quiz

Name _____ Date _____

Migrating Creatures Big and Small
Chapter 2, "Sea Turtles on the Run"
Fill in the bubble beside the answer for each question.

1. A mother sea turtle nests
   Ⓐ in grasses close to the beach.
   ● on the same beach she was born on.
   Ⓒ away from bright lights.

2. The first 100 feet of the turtle's migration
   ● is the hardest part of its trip.
   Ⓑ is the safest part of its trip.
   Ⓒ is the fastest part of its trip.

3. Only a few baby sea turtles
   Ⓐ get lost.
   Ⓑ get eaten.
   ● make it to the sea.

4. Some people try to help the sea turtles
   Ⓐ by tagging the male turtles.
   Ⓑ by putting tags on one of their legs.
   ● by making the beaches safe for the baby turtles.

Read the question, and write your answer.

Why do you think baby turtles start their trip at night? **Idea: The darkness of night would help protect them from animals that might eat them.**

Discovery • Book 6 75

Migrating Creatures Big and Small

Chapter Quiz

Name _____ Date _____

Migrating Creatures Big and Small
Chapter 3, "The Loon Family"
Mark each statement *T* for true or *F* for false.

F 1. The loon has black and white spots, a black head, and black eyes.
F 2. In the summer, the loon's home is in warmer places near the ocean.
T 3. Getting into the air is hard for the loon.
F 4. A good spot for a loon's nest is in trees near the shore.
T 5. The mother loon lays two eggs.
F 6. The loon parents fly south together for the winter.
T 7. The loon parents come back to the same nest in the spring.
F 8. The young loons leave with their parents in late fall.
T 9. Young loons won't go north again until they are three years old.
T 10. The loon has five major calls.

Read the question, and write your answer.

What are the meanings of the loon's calls? **joy, love, warning, anger, and "all's well"**

76 Discovery • Book 6

Migrating Creatures Big and Small

82 Discovery • Book 6

Answer Key

Chapter Quiz

Name _____ Date _____

Migrating Creatures Big and Small
Chapter 4, "The Monarch Butterfly"

Fill in the bubble beside the answer for each question.

1. Monarch butterflies
   - ● lay their eggs only on milkweed plants.
   - Ⓑ are found in the western part of Canada and the United States.
   - Ⓒ fly all the way to Mexico in the spring.

2. The monarch travels
   - Ⓐ up to 2,000 miles each year.
   - Ⓑ farther than any bird.
   - ● farther than any other butterfly.

3. The Mexican fir tree
   - Ⓐ helps the butterflies lay their eggs in the fall.
   - ● is the monarch's best spot to land.
   - Ⓒ covers over 2,000 square miles of Mexico today.

4. Young monarchs
   - Ⓐ follow their parents to the same spot each year.
   - Ⓑ always go back to the same tree each year.
   - ● go to the same spot their parents were the spring before.

Read the question, and write your answer.

What is one thing you would like to learn about monarch butterflies?
Answers will vary.

Chapter Quiz

Name _____ Date _____

Migrating Creatures Big and Small
Chapter 5, "Where Can the Bison Roam?"

Mark each statement T for true or F for false.

T 1. Bison are one of the biggest land animals.
T 2. Bison begin their migration at Yellowstone National Park.
F 3. Bison travel 200 miles each way.
T 4. Bison with tags can be tracked.
T 5. Boris was a bison whose tag fell off.
F 6. Because bison are big, migration is not hard.
T 7. The state of Montana has rules about where bison can go.
F 8. The rules help bison know where they can go.
T 9. Sometimes the bison at Yellowstone get too close to people.
T 10. Bison do not have a place to safely roam.

Read the question, and write your answer.

Why do you think the bison is one of the United States' most loved animals?
Idea: Bison are one of the biggest land animals that live in the wild in the United States.

Chapter Quiz

Name _____ Date _____

Migrating Creatures Big and Small
Chapter 6, "Trout Making a Splash"

Fill in the bubble beside the answer for each question.

1. Trout that live in both freshwater and salt water
   - Ⓐ are the biggest trout.
   - ● are called "sea-run" trout.
   - Ⓒ lay their eggs in shallow parts of the ocean.

2. Trout migrate
   - ● using their sense of smell to guide them.
   - Ⓑ to the ocean to lay their eggs.
   - Ⓒ from coasts to deep parts of the ocean.

3. Trout lay their eggs
   - ● in the place where they were born.
   - Ⓑ in deep waters.
   - Ⓒ in warm waters.

4. What happens when trout run into a waterfall on their way?
   - Ⓐ They find a different way to go.
   - Ⓑ They know of ways that don't have waterfalls.
   - ● They keep leaping until they make it to the top of the waterfall.

Read the question, and write your answer.

Why do trout that live in the ocean have to migrate? **They must find smaller waters in which to lay their eggs.**

Thinking and Writing

Name _____ Date _____

Migrating Creatures Big and Small
Think About It

Write about or give an oral presentation for each question.

1. Choose two animals from this book. Compare their migrations. How are they similar? How are they different?
   Accept reasonable responses.

2. Name ways that migration helps animals. **Ideas: The hummingbird and monarch migrate because they cannot survive cold temperatures. The sea turtle and trout migrate to lay their eggs.**

3. Name one way people cause problems for migrating animals.
   Ideas: In Mexico, people need wood and cut down the fir trees that monarchs need. Bright lights can cause sea turtles to get lost. Bison sometimes get too close to cars and get hurt.

4. What is one way tagging helps animals? **Ideas: People began protecting the Mexican fir tree because they learned how important it was to the monarch. Tagging sea turtles helps people protect the beaches turtles use to lay their eggs.**

Write About It

Choose one of the questions below. Write your answer on a sheet of paper.

1. Pretend you work at Yellowstone National Park. What rules would you make to protect the bison?

2. If you could help tag one of the animals mentioned in this book, which one would it be? Give reasons for your answer.

3. Complete the Content Web for this book.

Migrating Creatures Big and Small

Building Background

Name _____ Date _____

The Prince and the Beggar
What You Know

Write answers to these questions.

1. Where would you like to live? Name some things this place would have.
   _____

2. A crown is a sign of royalty. What are some other symbols of royalty? (Hint: You might find it helpful to look at pictures of kings and queens to answer this question.) _____
   _____

3. Is there a famous person you would like to meet? Why would you like to meet this person? _____
   _____

4. What is a royal seal? How does a seal work? _____
   _____

Word Meanings
Definitions

Look for these words as you read your chapter book. When you find one of these words, write its definition.

beggar: _____

crown: _____

kingdom: _____

palace: _____

sword: _____

town: _____

84   Discovery • Book 7

Word Lists

The Prince and the Beggar

Unfamiliar Words	Word Meanings	Proper Nouns	
knew, prince	beggar, town	Andrew, Edward Tutor, John Canty, London	Chapter 1
apart, color, face, great, large, pies, poor, soldiers, thought	palace		Chapter 2
lord	crown	England	Chapter 3
chase, crowd, otherwise, straw	sword		Chapter 4
		Miles Hendon	Chapter 5
friend, throne	kingdom		Chapter 6

Discovery • Book 7

Chapter Quiz

Name _____ Date _____

The Prince and the Beggar
Chapter 1, "A Prince Is Born"

Mark each statement *T* for true or *F* for false.

____ 1. When the prince was born, bells rang and people sang in the streets.

____ 2. The prince was named Edward Tutor.

____ 3. The king was proud to have a son.

____ 4. When Tom Canty was born, he was as lucky as the prince.

____ 5. John Canty was very happy when Tom was born.

____ 6. John had to beg for more food when Tom was born.

____ 7. Tom never begged for food.

____ 8. Because Tom was a beggar, he did not learn to read and write.

____ 9. Tom always walked with his head bent low.

____ 10. What Tom wanted most of all was to meet a real prince.

Read the question, and write your answer.

Compare the way the king acted when the prince was born to the way John acted when Tom was born. _____

_____

_____

Chapter Quiz

Name _____ Date _____

The Prince and the Beggar
Chapter 2, "Tom Meets the Prince"

Number the events in order from 1 to 5.

___ The prince gave Tom some food.

___ Tom saw a boy inside the palace gate.

___ The prince told Tom to come with him.

___ Tom saw that he and the prince were about the same size.

___ A soldier grabbed Tom and sent him spinning to the ground.

Number the events in order from 6 to 10.

___ Prince Edward picked up his father's Great Seal.

___ The prince and Tom exchanged clothes.

___ The prince was grabbed by one of the soldiers and tossed outside the palace gate.

___ Tom told the prince what he did for fun.

___ Tom told the prince he only had the clothes he was wearing.

Read the question, and write your answer.

What do you think will happen next? _____

_____

_____

Discovery • Book 7

Chapter Quiz

Name _____ Date _____

The Prince and the Beggar
Chapter 3, "Tom at the Palace"

Fill in the bubble beside the answer for each question.

1. What did Tom do while he waited for the prince to return?
   - Ⓐ He explored the palace.
   - Ⓑ He walked around in shoes that made his feet hurt.
   - Ⓒ He ate all the prince's food.

2. What did the girl who saw Tom dressed as the prince think had happened?
   - Ⓐ She thought the prince had gone mad.
   - Ⓑ She thought the prince had been kidnapped.
   - Ⓒ She thought the prince was playing a joke on her.

3. What did King Henry look like?
   - Ⓐ He was a tall man dressed in purple and gold.
   - Ⓑ He was small and weak, and he looked tired.
   - Ⓒ He was a big man with white whiskers.

4. What did King Henry ask Tom to bring?
   - Ⓐ a chair for him to rest his leg on
   - Ⓑ some paper
   - Ⓒ the Great Seal

Read the question, and write your answer.

Why did the lords start to make plans to crown Tom king of England?

_____

_____

Chapter Quiz

Name _____ Date _____

The Prince and the Beggar
Chapter 4, "Edward Sees England"

Number the events in order from 1 to 5.

____ A man in rags grabbed Edward.

____ Outside the gates, Edward yelled, "I am the prince!"

____ Edward slept on dirty straw.

____ John thought his son had gone mad.

____ Edward followed a crowd through the streets.

Mark each statement *T* for true or *F* for false.

____ 1. Edward saw Tom being crowned.

____ 2. The crowd believed Edward.

____ 3. The crowd began to chase Edward.

____ 4. The tall man offered to help Edward.

Read the question, and write your answer.

Why do you think the tall man helped Edward? _____

_____

_____

Discovery • Book 7

Chapter Quiz

Name _____ Date _____

The Prince and the Beggar
Chapter 5, "Miles Hendon"

Mark each statement *T* for true or *F* for false.

____ 1. The tall man was named Miles Hendon.

____ 2. Edward and Miles sat together to eat a meal.

____ 3. Miles let Edward have the bed.

____ 4. Edward agreed to let Miles sit.

____ 5. Miles thought Edward would be okay by himself.

____ 6. Miles decided to take Edward with him.

____ 7. Edward refused to go with Miles.

____ 8. Edward talked to the people he met.

____ 9. Edward thought he would help the poor when he became king.

____ 10. Edward returned to London by himself.

Read the question, and write your answer.

What did Prince Edward learn about the people of England when he was with Miles? _____

_____

_____

Chapter Quiz

Name _____ Date _____

The Prince and the Beggar
Chapter 6, "A King Is Crowned"

Fill in the bubble beside the answer for each question.

1. What did Tom think as he looked at the people?
   - Ⓐ He thought they looked very poor.
   - Ⓑ He thought about how unlucky he was.
   - Ⓒ He thought he might become the king.

2. What did the lords begin to see when Tom and Edward stood close together?
   - Ⓐ The boys looked like each other.
   - Ⓑ Tom did not look like the real prince.
   - Ⓒ A change had come over Edward.

3. What was Edward unable to remember?
   - Ⓐ many things about King Henry and the palace
   - Ⓑ who the lords were
   - Ⓒ where he had put the Great Seal

4. What did the new king say about Tom and Miles?
   - Ⓐ He said they would need his help.
   - Ⓑ He said they had helped him get his kingdom back.
   - Ⓒ He said they should be allowed to go home.

Read the question, and write your answer.

How did Tom help Edward remember where he had put the Great Seal?

_____

_____

Thinking and Writing

Name _____ Date _____

The Prince and the Beggar
Think About It

Write about or give an oral presentation for each question.

1. What does the following saying mean? *The grass is always greener on the other side of the fence.* How do you think Tom and Edward might have felt about this saying? _____
_____
_____

2. Why would no one believe the boys when they said they were not who they appeared to be? _____
_____
_____

3. How do you think Edward's time as a beggar might change the way he will rule as a king? _____
_____
_____

4. If you could trade places with someone for one day, who would it be? Why? _____
_____
_____

Write About It

Choose one of the questions below. Write your answer on a sheet of paper.

1. Pretend you are Prince Edward. Write a thank you letter to Miles.

2. The Great Seal is lost! Write a Lost and Found column for the newspaper. Start by describing what is lost. Offer a reward if the seal is found. Make sure you tell your readers how to contact you.

3. Complete the Compare and Contrast Diagram for this book.

92   Discovery • Book 7

Fluency Passages

The Prince and the Beggar

Chapter 1 *page 4*

*Tom met a good man on the streets. His name was Andrew, and he	14
helped children. He showed them how to read and write. And he told them	28
stories about the lives of kings and princes.	36
Tom loved these stories. He loved to hear about how they lived and	49
what they ate.	52
After a while, Tom knew so much about* princes that he began to	65
think he *was* one. Tom washed himself in the river. He talked like a prince.	80
He walked with his head high.	86

Chapter 6 *pages 24 and 25*

*Tom sat on a throne in a hall filled with people dressed in fine	14
clothes. Somebody was just about to put the crown on his head.	26
Just then, a little beggar boy slipped past the soldiers. He ran	38
through the great hall, waving his hands.	45
"Don't put that crown on his head!" he shouted. "I am Prince	57
Edward!"	58
The soldiers* grabbed Edward.	62
"Let him go!" Tom shouted. He stood and said, "He is the real king."	76
The beggar boy moved closer to the throne. The lords began to see	89
how much he looked like the prince.	96

- The target rate for **Discovery** is 60 wcpm. The asterisks (*) mark 60 words.
- Listen to the student read the passage. Count the number of words read in one minute and the number of errors.
- For the reading rate, subtract the number of errors from the total number of words read.
- Have students enter their scores on their **Fluency Graph.** See page 9.

Discovery • Book 7

Answer Key

Building Background

Name _____ Date _____

The Prince and the Beggar
What You Know
Write answers to these questions.

1. Where would you like to live? Name some things this place would have. **Accept reasonable responses.**

2. A crown is a sign of royalty. What are some other symbols of royalty? (Hint: You might find it helpful to look at pictures of kings and queens to answer this question.) **Ideas: scepter, orb, throne, the color red or purple, expensive clothing and jewelry, a cape or mantle**

3. Is there a famous person you would like to meet? Why would you like to meet this person? **Answers will vary. Ideas: for a photograph or autograph; to thank that person; to get that person's advice**

4. What is a royal seal? How does a seal work? **A royal seal is the official stamp of a king or queen. It is used to show that kings or queens agree with an official document.**

Word Meanings
Definitions
Look for these words as you read your chapter book. When you find one of these words, write its definition.

beggar: **a person who lives by asking others for money, clothes, or food**
crown: **to make one a king or queen by putting a crown on him or her**
kingdom: **a country ruled by a king or queen**
palace: **the official house of a ruler, usually a large, grand building**
sword: **a weapon that has a long, sharp blade with a hilt, or handle, at one end**
town: **a place that is larger than a village but smaller than a city and contains houses, stores, and other buildings**

84

Chapter Quiz

Name _____ Date _____

The Prince and the Beggar
Chapter 1, "A Prince Is Born"

Mark each statement *T* for true or *F* for false.

T 1. When the prince was born, bells rang and people sang in the streets.
T 2. The prince was named Edward Tutor.
T 3. The king was proud to have a son.
F 4. When Tom Canty was born, he was as lucky as the prince.
F 5. John Canty was very happy when Tom was born.
T 6. John had to beg for more food when Tom was born.
F 7. Tom never begged for food.
F 8. Because Tom was a beggar, he did not learn to read and write.
F 9. Tom always walked with his head bent low.
T 10. What Tom wanted most of all was to meet a real prince.

Read the question, and write your answer.

Compare the way the king acted when the prince was born to the way John acted when Tom was born. **The king acted happy and proud when the prince was born. John said he had another mouth to feed when Tom was born. He slammed the door when he went out to beg. He was acting worried and a little angry.**

86

Chapter Quiz

Name _____ Date _____

The Prince and the Beggar
Chapter 2, "Tom Meets the Prince"

Number the events in order from 1 to 5.

4 The prince gave Tom some food.
1 Tom saw a boy inside the palace gate.
3 The prince told Tom to come with him.
5 Tom saw that he and the prince were about the same size.
2 A soldier grabbed Tom and sent him spinning to the ground.

Number the events in order from 6 to 10.

7 Prince Edward picked up his father's Great Seal.
9 The prince and Tom exchanged clothes.
10 The prince was grabbed by one of the soldiers and tossed outside the palace gate.
8 Tom told the prince what he did for fun.
6 Tom told the prince he only had the clothes he was wearing.

Read the question, and write your answer.
What do you think will happen next? **Answers will vary.**

87

Chapter Quiz

Name _____ Date _____

The Prince and the Beggar
Chapter 3, "Tom at the Palace"

Fill in the bubble beside the answer for each question.

1. What did Tom do while he waited for the prince to return?
   Ⓐ He explored the palace.
   ● He walked around in shoes that made his feet hurt.
   Ⓒ He ate all the prince's food.

2. What did the girl who saw Tom dressed as the prince think had happened?
   ● She thought the prince had gone mad.
   Ⓑ She thought the prince had been kidnapped.
   Ⓒ She thought the prince was playing a joke on her.

3. What did King Henry look like?
   Ⓐ He was a tall man dressed in purple and gold.
   Ⓑ He was small and weak, and he looked tired.
   ● He was a big man with white whiskers.

4. What did King Henry ask Tom to bring?
   Ⓐ a chair for him to rest his leg on
   Ⓑ some paper
   ● the Great Seal

Read the question, and write your answer.

Why did the lords start to make plans to crown Tom king of England? **When King Henry died, the country needed a new king. Prince Edward was supposed to be the new king. No one knew or believed that Tom and the prince had switched places.**

88

---

94   Discovery • Book 7

# Answer Key

Chapter Quiz

Name _____ Date _____

The Prince and the Beggar
Chapter 4, "Edward Sees England"
Number the events in order from 1 to 5.

__2__ A man in rags grabbed Edward.
__1__ Outside the gates, Edward yelled, "I am the prince!"
__4__ Edward slept on dirty straw.
__3__ John thought his son had gone mad.
__5__ Edward followed a crowd through the streets.

Mark each statement *T* for true or *F* for false.

__F__ 1. Edward saw Tom being crowned.
__F__ 2. The crowd believed Edward.
__T__ 3. The crowd began to chase Edward.
__T__ 4. The tall man offered to help Edward.

Read the question, and write your answer.

Why do you think the tall man helped Edward? **Ideas: He saw a crowd chasing Edward; he probably felt sorry for Edward.**

Discovery • Book 7   89

The Prince and the Beggar

Chapter Quiz

Name _____ Date _____

The Prince and the Beggar
Chapter 5, "Miles Hendon"
Mark each statement *T* for true or *F* for false.

__T__ 1. The tall man was named Miles Hendon.
__F__ 2. Edward and Miles sat together to eat a meal.
__T__ 3. Miles let Edward have the bed.
__T__ 4. Edward agreed to let Miles sit.
__F__ 5. Miles thought Edward would be okay by himself.
__T__ 6. Miles decided to take Edward with him.
__F__ 7. Edward refused to go with Miles.
__T__ 8. Edward talked to the people he met.
__T__ 9. Edward thought he would help the poor when he became king.
__F__ 10. Edward returned to London by himself.

Read the question, and write your answer.

What did Prince Edward learn about the people of England when he was with Miles? **The prince learned that many of the people of England were very poor.**

90   Discovery • Book 7

The Prince and the Beggar

Chapter Quiz

Name _____ Date _____

The Prince and the Beggar
Chapter 6, "A King Is Crowned"
Fill in the bubble beside the answer for each question.

1. What did Tom think as he looked at the people?
   Ⓐ He thought they looked very poor.
   Ⓑ He thought about how unlucky he was.
   ● He thought he might become the king.

2. What did the lords begin to see when Tom and Edward stood close together?
   ● The boys looked like each other.
   Ⓑ Tom did not look like the real prince.
   Ⓒ A change had come over Edward.

3. What was Edward unable to remember?
   Ⓐ many things about King Henry and the palace
   Ⓑ who the lords were
   ● where he had put the Great Seal

4. What did the new king say about Tom and Miles?
   Ⓐ He said they would need his help.
   ● He said they had helped him get his kingdom back.
   Ⓒ He said they should be allowed to go home.

Read the question, and write your answer.

How did Tom help Edward remember where he had put the Great Seal? **Tom reminded Edward about the things he had done after they had traded clothes. He said Edward had been about to go outside with the Great Seal in his hand.**

Discovery • Book 7   91

The Prince and the Beggar

Thinking and Writing

Name _____ Date _____

The Prince and the Beggar
Think About It
Write about or give an oral presentation for each question.

1. What does the following saying mean? *The grass is always greener on the other side of the fence.* How do you think Tom and Edward might have felt about this saying? **This saying means that sometimes you think other people are better off than you. Tom and Edward felt that way in the beginning of the story, but changed as they had new experiences.**

2. Why would no one believe the boys when they said they were not who they appeared to be? **The boys looked alike and had exchanged clothes.**

3. How do you think Edward's time as a beggar might change the way he will rule as a king? **Ideas: Edward will help the poor in his country; Edward will listen to his people.**

4. If you could trade places with someone for one day, who would it be? Why? **Answers will vary.**

Write About It
Choose one of the questions below. Write your answer on a sheet of paper.

1. Pretend you are Prince Edward. Write a thank you letter to Miles.
2. The Great Seal is lost! Write a Lost and Found column for the newspaper. Start by describing what is lost. Offer a reward if the seal is found. Make sure you tell your readers how to contact you.
3. Complete the Compare and Contrast Diagram for this book.

92   Discovery • Book 7

The Prince and the Beggar

Discovery • Book 7   95

Building Background

Name _____ Date _____

Swiss Family Robinson
What You Know

Write answers to these questions.

1. Have you ever climbed a tree or been in a tree house? What was it like?

   _____

   _____

2. Research to find out where coconut trees grow. Name some of the places. Describe their climates. _____

   _____

3. What kinds of animals make good pets? Which animals are helpful to humans? _____

Word Meanings
Matching

Look for these words as you read your chapter book. When you find a word, draw a line to connect the word with the correct definition.

bamboo	being in an early part of life or growth
coward	a very large bird of Africa and southwestern Asia, with a long neck and long legs that runs swiftly and cannot fly
monkey	a small telescope
ostrich	a person who has no courage or is easily frightened
spyglass	one of a group of furry animals that usually have flat, hairless faces and long tails; they are primates and have hands and feet that can grasp things
young	a tropical plant with woody stems that are hollow and jointed; it is a kind of grass that grows as tall as trees

96   Discovery • Book 8

Word Lists

Swiss Family Robinson

Unfamiliar Words	Word Meanings	Proper Nouns	
captain, change	coward	Ernest, Franz, Fritz, Switzerland	Chapter 1
coconut, island, wrongs	spyglass		Chapter 2
built, honey, shelter	bamboo	Falconhurst	Chapter 3
friends, parrot	monkey		Chapter 4
donkey, medals, race	ostrich		Chapter 5
exploring, good-bye, knew, lonely, pretended, rescued, understood, whole	young	Edward, Jenny Montrose, British	Chapter 6

Discovery • Book 8

97

Chapter Quiz

Name _____ Date _____

Swiss Family Robinson
Chapter 1, "The Storm"

Fill in the bubble beside the answer for each question.

1. Why was the family on a ship?
   - Ⓐ The boys were learning how to become sailors.
   - Ⓑ They were bringing things from Switzerland to a new country.
   - Ⓒ They were taking a trip to Switzerland.

2. What did the family have on board the ship?
   - Ⓐ plants, food, and animals
   - Ⓑ enough money to get back home
   - Ⓒ Swiss-made trading goods

3. What happened when the captain yelled, "We are lost"?
   - Ⓐ The family went below.
   - Ⓑ The sailors began to jump off the boat.
   - Ⓒ The family got into the last lifeboat.

4. When the storm finally ended,
   - Ⓐ the family planned what to do next.
   - Ⓑ the captain surveyed the damage.
   - Ⓒ the family was so tired no one could even speak.

Read the question, and write your answer.

What do you think will happen in the next chapter? _____
_____
_____

Chapter Quiz

Name _____ Date _____

Swiss Family Robinson
Chapter 2, "Island Ho!"

Number the events in order from 1 to 5.

____ Turk jumped in the water.

____ The ship was stuck between two big rocks.

____ The family floated to shore in four wooden tubs.

____ Fritz woke to animal sounds.

____ They cheered when they reached the sandy beach.

Mark each statement *T* for true or *F* for false.

____ 1. Franz could see tall coconut trees through a spyglass.

____ 2. Father decided they should stay together for safety.

____ 3. Franz hoped some of the sailors were on the island.

____ 4. Father thought they might need the help of the sailors.

Read the question, and write your answer.

Why did the family decide to leave the animals on the ship? _____

_____

_____

Discovery • Book 8

Chapter Quiz

Name _____ Date _____

Swiss Family Robinson
Chapter 3, "Falconhurst"

Fill in the bubble beside the answer for each question.

1. Mother felt the best plan for a safe home was
   - Ⓐ deep in the woods.
   - Ⓑ near a wide stream.
   - Ⓒ a tree house.

2. Their new home was
   - Ⓐ made of sticks, leaves, and branches.
   - Ⓑ finished within three weeks.
   - Ⓒ both A and B

3. Why did the bees come after the family?
   - Ⓐ They had taken the bees' home.
   - Ⓑ They had cut off the branches where the bees lived.
   - Ⓒ They had raided the bees' hive for honey.

4. What was at the very top of the family's home?
   - Ⓐ branches and leaves
   - Ⓑ a large window for watching the stars
   - Ⓒ a small deck

Read the question, and write your answer.

Why did the family name their home Falconhurst? _____

_____

_____

Chapter Quiz

Name _____ Date _____

Swiss Family Robinson
Chapter 4, "Monkey See, Monkey Do"

Mark each statement *T* for true or *F* for false.

_____ 1. Father and Fritz came upon monkeys in the coconut trees.

_____ 2. Father said coconuts had sour but refreshing juice inside them.

_____ 3. Father and Fritz threw rocks into the trees.

_____ 4. The monkeys threw the coconuts to the ground.

_____ 5. Father and Fritz did not take any coconuts home.

_____ 6. Fritz found a baby monkey and named him Max.

_____ 7. Ernest trained a green parrot.

_____ 8. Jack found a horse and named her Bella.

_____ 9. Turk was the animal Franz liked best.

_____ 10. The animals the children found ran away from them.

Read the question, and write your answer.

Which of the animals they found do you think would be most helpful?

_____

_____

_____

Discovery • Book 8

Chapter Quiz

Name _____ Date _____

Swiss Family Robinson
Chapter 5, "Let the Games Begin"

Number the events in order from 1 to 5.

____ Turk and Max won the relay.

____ Jack and Ernest thought the animals should race each other.

____ They had a contest to see who could find the most clams.

____ Father lined everyone up.

____ Mother handed the winners shiny medals.

Mark each statement *T* for true or *F* for false.

____ 1. Mother found the medals on the ship.

____ 2. At the end of the day they put the animals in caves.

____ 3. Mother made flat bread and sweet apples for supper.

____ 4. This was one of their best days on the island.

Read the question, and write your answer.

Why do you think this was one of their best days on the island? _____

_____

_____

Chapter Quiz

Name _____ Date _____

Swiss Family Robinson
Chapter 6, "My Grand Find," and Afterword

Mark each statement *T* for true or *F* for false.

___ 1. When Fritz turned 23, he decided to leave the island.

___ 2. Fritz left to explore his favorite parts of the island.

___ 3. Father came looking for Fritz after two weeks.

___ 4. While Fritz was fishing, he found another person.

___ 5. Fritz and Edward became friends.

___ 6. Edward was one of the sailors who had been on the ship with the family.

___ 7. Fritz and Jenny fell in love with each other.

___ 8. Father and Mother Robinson stayed on the island for the rest of their lives.

___ 9. Fritz and Jenny made a map to the island.

___ 10. Fritz and Jenny were never able to return to the island.

Read the question, and write your answer.

Why did Fritz and Jenny go to England? _____

_____

_____

Discovery • Book 8

Thinking and Writing

Name _____ Date _____

Swiss Family Robinson
Think About It

Write about or give an oral presentation for each question.

1. Why do you think the sailors abandoned the ship? _____
   _____

2. What were the advantages of building a house in a tree? What were the disadvantages? Explain your answer. _____
   _____
   _____

3. What qualities did the Robinson family have that made them successful on the island? _____
   _____

4. Why do you think Fritz always wanted to stay when he returned to the island? _____
   _____
   _____

Write About It

Choose one of the questions below. Write your answer on a sheet of paper.

1. If you were stranded on an island, what things would you need to survive?

2. Pretend you are going to begin living in a place where no one else lives. Plan the things you would take with you. Explain your choices.

3. Write a journal entry for Father or Mother Robinson after Fritz and Jenny left the island.

4. Complete the Book Report Form for this book.

Fluency Passages

Swiss Family Robinson

Chapter 2 *page 6*

*I woke to animal sounds. My dog, Turk, licked my hand. I walked	13
up on deck.	16
In the warm sunlight, I saw that our ship was stuck between two big	30
rocks. And land was not far away! The rocks had saved our lives. Had we	45
jumped into the sea with the sailors, we would have died.	56
After looking things over,* Father came up with a plan. We found	68
four wooden tubs. We dropped them into the water. These tubs would	80
float us safely to shore.	85

Chapter 5 *page 18*

*Ernest's ostrich took a few big leaps. Then it went around and	12
around in the sand, making Ernest sick. The cow never moved. So Jack	25
left her and grabbed a pig. At first he seemed to be riding the pig. But	41
then we saw that he was carrying it! My donkey didn't move at all.	55
Turk and Max won the* relay with no help from any of us.	68
We ran more races the rest of the day. We also had a contest to see	84
who could find the most clams.	90

- The target rate for **Discovery** is 60 wcpm. The asterisks (*) mark 60 words.
- Listen to the student read the passage. Count the number of words read in one minute and the number of errors.
- For the reading rate, subtract the number of errors from the total number of words read.
- Have students enter their scores on their **Fluency Graph.** See page 9.

Answer Key

Building Background

Name _____ Date _____

Swiss Family Robinson
What You Know

Write answers to these questions.

1. Have you ever climbed a tree or been in a tree house? What was it like?
   Answers will vary.

2. Research to find out where coconut trees grow. Name some of the places. Describe their climates. **Ideas: along warm sea coasts, Indonesia, Philippines, South Pacific and Caribbean islands, Hawaii; warm, tropical climates**

3. What kinds of animals make good pets? Which animals are helpful to humans? **Ideas: dogs, cats; horses, donkeys, oxen**

Word Meanings
Matching

Look for these words as you read your chapter book. When you find a word, draw a line to connect the word with the correct definition.

- bamboo — a tropical plant with woody stems that are hollow and jointed; it is a kind of grass that grows as tall as trees
- coward — a person who has no courage or is easily frightened
- monkey — one of a group of furry animals that usually have flat, hairless faces and long tails; they are primates and have hands and feet that can grasp things
- ostrich — a very large bird of Africa and southwestern Asia, with a long neck and long legs that runs swiftly and cannot fly
- spyglass — a small telescope
- young — being in an early part of life or growth

96 — Discovery • Book 8

Swiss Family Robinson

Chapter Quiz

Name _____ Date _____

Swiss Family Robinson
Chapter 1, "The Storm"

Fill in the bubble beside the answer for each question.

1. Why was the family on a ship?
   - Ⓐ The boys were learning how to become sailors.
   - ● They were bringing things from Switzerland to a new country.
   - Ⓒ They were taking a trip to Switzerland.

2. What did the family have on board the ship?
   - ● plants, food, and animals
   - Ⓑ enough money to get back home
   - Ⓒ Swiss-made trading goods

3. What happened when the captain yelled, "We are lost"?
   - Ⓐ The family went below.
   - ● The sailors began to jump off the boat.
   - Ⓒ The family got into the last lifeboat.

4. When the storm finally ended,
   - Ⓐ the family planned what to do next.
   - Ⓑ the captain surveyed the damage.
   - ● the family was so tired no one could even speak.

Read the question, and write your answer.

What do you think will happen in the next chapter? _____
Answers will vary.

98 — Discovery • Book 8

Swiss Family Robinson

Chapter Quiz

Name _____ Date _____

Swiss Family Robinson
Chapter 2, "Island Ho!"

Number the events in order from 1 to 5.

- _4_ Turk jumped in the water.
- _2_ The ship was stuck between two big rocks.
- _3_ The family floated to shore in four wooden tubs.
- _1_ Fritz woke to animal sounds.
- _5_ They cheered when they reached the sandy beach.

Mark each statement T for true or F for false.

- _T_ 1. Franz could see tall coconut trees through a spyglass.
- _F_ 2. Father decided they should stay together for safety.
- _F_ 3. Franz hoped some of the sailors were on the island.
- _T_ 4. Father thought they might need the help of the sailors.

Read the question, and write your answer.

Why did the family decide to leave the animals on the ship? _____
They had no way to get the animals safely to shore.

Discovery • Book 8 — 99

Swiss Family Robinson

Chapter Quiz

Name _____ Date _____

Swiss Family Robinson
Chapter 3, "Falconhurst"

Fill in the bubble beside the answer for each question.

1. Mother felt the best plan for a safe home was
   - Ⓐ deep in the woods.
   - Ⓑ near a wide stream.
   - ● a tree house.

2. Their new home was
   - Ⓐ made of sticks, leaves, and branches.
   - Ⓑ finished within three weeks.
   - ● both A and B

3. Why did the bees come after the family?
   - ● They had taken the bees' home.
   - Ⓑ They had cut off the branches where the bees lived.
   - Ⓒ They had raided the bees' hive for honey.

4. What was at the very top of the family's home?
   - Ⓐ branches and leaves
   - Ⓑ a large window for watching the stars
   - ● a small deck

Read the question, and write your answer.

Why did the family name their home Falconhurst? **Ideas: A falcon is a kind of bird; they were like birds in a nest in the house built in a tree.**

100 — Discovery • Book 8

Swiss Family Robinson

---

106 — Discovery • Book 8

# Answer Key

Chapter Quiz

Name _____ Date _____

Swiss Family Robinson
Chapter 4, "Monkey See, Monkey Do"

Mark each statement *T* for true or *F* for false.

- **T** 1. Father and Fritz came upon monkeys in the coconut trees.
- **F** 2. Father said coconuts had sour but refreshing juice inside them.
- **T** 3. Father and Fritz threw rocks into the trees.
- **F** 4. The monkeys threw the coconuts to the ground.
- **F** 5. Father and Fritz did not take any coconuts home.
- **T** 6. Fritz found a baby monkey and named him Max.
- **T** 7. Ernest trained a green parrot.
- **T** 8. Jack found a horse and named her Bella.
- **F** 9. Turk was the animal Franz liked best.
- **F** 10. The animals the children found ran away from them.

Read the question, and write your answer.

Which of the animals they found do you think would be most helpful?
Ideas: the horse, the monkey

Discovery • Book 8 — 101
Swiss Family Robinson

Chapter Quiz

Name _____ Date _____

Swiss Family Robinson
Chapter 5, "Let the Games Begin"

Number the events in order from 1 to 5.

- **3** Turk and Max won the relay.
- **1** Jack and Ernest thought the animals should race each other.
- **4** They had a contest to see who could find the most clams.
- **2** Father lined everyone up.
- **5** Mother handed the winners shiny medals.

Mark each statement *T* for true or *F* for false.

- **T** 1. Mother found the medals on the ship.
- **F** 2. At the end of the day they put the animals in caves.
- **T** 3. Mother made flat bread and sweet apples for supper.
- **T** 4. This was one of their best days on the island.

Read the question, and write your answer.

Why do you think this was one of their best days on the island?
Ideas: The animals did funny things; the family played games; they laughed and had fun; they had good food to eat.

102 — Discovery • Book 8
Swiss Family Robinson

Chapter Quiz

Name _____ Date _____

Swiss Family Robinson
Chapter 6, "My Grand Find," and Afterword

Mark each statement *T* for true or *F* for false.

- **F** 1. When Fritz turned 23, he decided to leave the island.
- **F** 2. Fritz left to explore his favorite parts of the island.
- **F** 3. Father came looking for Fritz after two weeks.
- **T** 4. While Fritz was fishing, he found another person.
- **T** 5. Fritz and Edward became friends.
- **F** 6. Edward was one of the sailors who had been on the ship with the family.
- **T** 7. Fritz and Jenny fell in love with each other.
- **T** 8. Father and Mother Robinson stayed on the island for the rest of their lives.
- **T** 9. Fritz and Jenny made a map to the island.
- **F** 10. Fritz and Jenny were never able to return to the island.

Read the question, and write your answer.

Why did Fritz and Jenny go to England? **to be with her father's family**

Discovery • Book 8 — 103
Swiss Family Robinson

Thinking and Writing

Name _____ Date _____

Swiss Family Robinson
Think About It

Write about or give an oral presentation for each question.

1. Why do you think the sailors abandoned the ship? **Ideas: They were scared; they thought they could save themselves by getting into the lifeboats.**

2. What were the advantages of building a house in a tree? What were the disadvantages? Explain your answer. **Ideas: Being off the ground offered protection from animals and intruders; it might be difficult to get down quickly and safely.**

3. What qualities did the Robinson family have that made them successful on the island? **Ideas: worked hard; were creative problem solvers; helped each other; took time to have fun**

4. Why do you think Fritz always wanted to stay when he returned to the island? **Ideas: had good memories; his parents were there; island felt like home**

Write About It

Choose one of the questions below. Write your answer on a sheet of paper.

1. If you were stranded on an island, what things would you need to survive?
2. Pretend you are going to begin living in a place where no one else lives. Plan the things you would take with you. Explain your choices.
3. Write a journal entry for Father or Mother Robinson after Fritz and Jenny left the island.
4. Complete the Book Report Form for this book.

104 — Discovery • Book 8
Swiss Family Robinson

Discovery • Book 8 — 107

Graphic Organizer

Name _____ Date _____

A Very Strange Place
Prediction/Outcome Chart

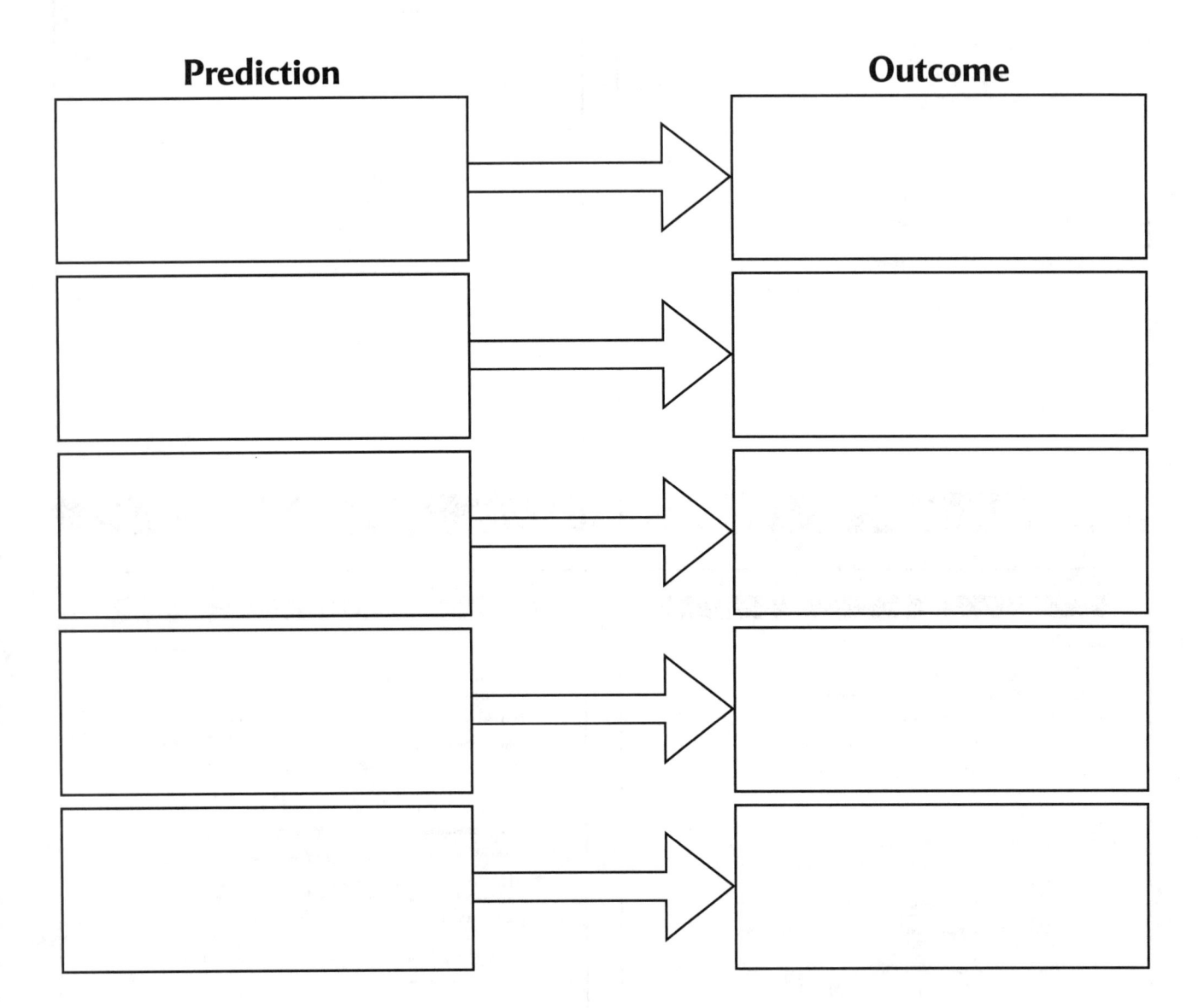

Prediction		Outcome
☐	→	☐
☐	→	☐
☐	→	☐
☐	→	☐
☐	→	☐

Graphic Organizer

Name _____ Date _____

Rebuilding Fun
Problem → Solution → Effect Chart

Problem

Solution

Effect

Discovery

Graphic Organizer

Name _____ Date _____

The Roof of the World
Main Idea/Details Chart

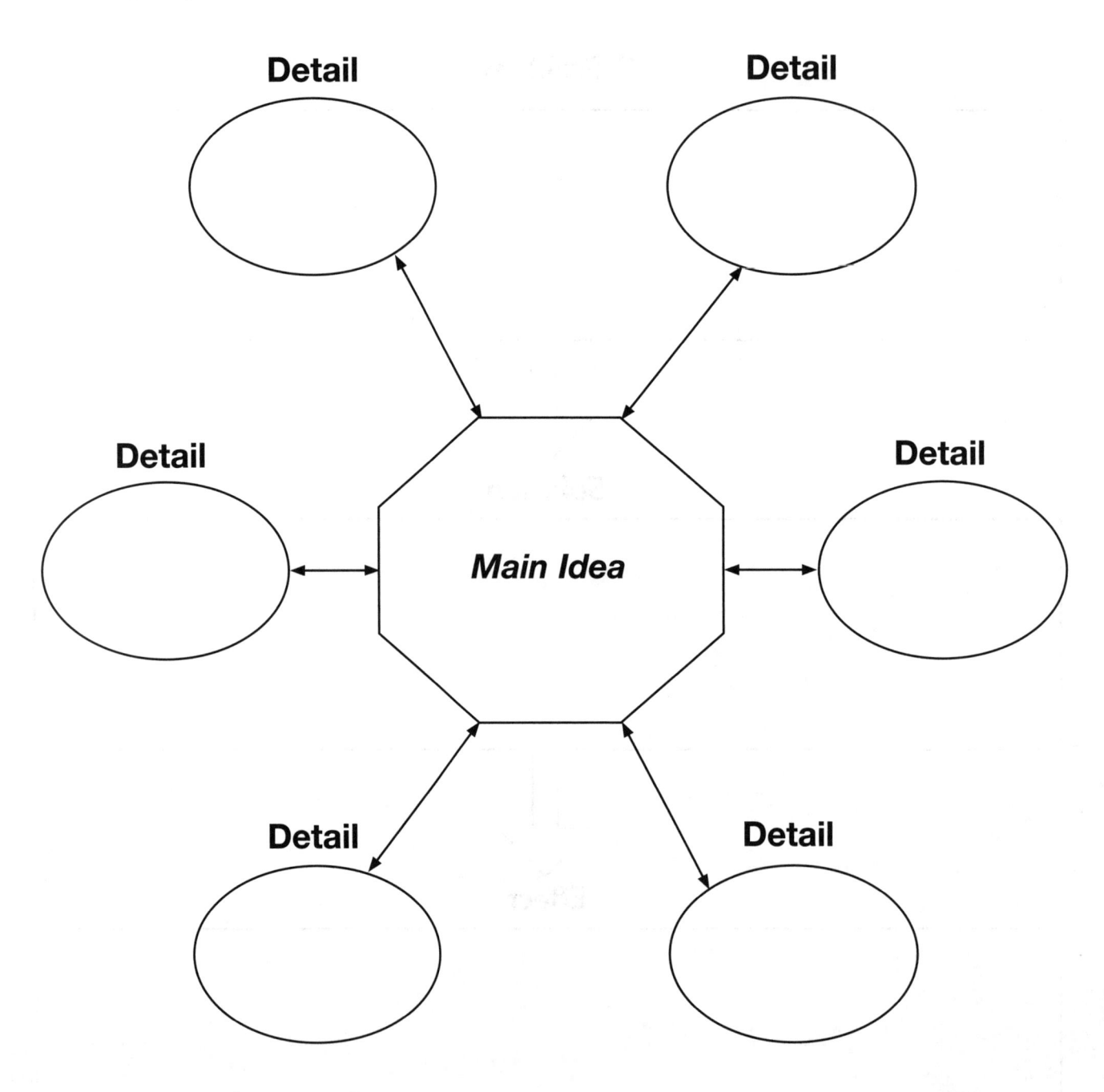

Detail

Detail

Detail

Main Idea

Detail

Detail

Detail

110 Discovery

Graphic Organizer

Name _____ Date _____

Stonehenge: A Very Special Place
Making Inferences Chart

What the Book Says:

Page #

Page #

Page #

Page #

What I Think:

Discovery

Graphic Organizer

Name _____ Date _____

Shipwrecks and Their Secrets
What I Know/What I Learned Chart

What I Know	What I Want to Know	What I Learned

Name _____ Date _____

Migrating Creatures Big and Small
Content Web

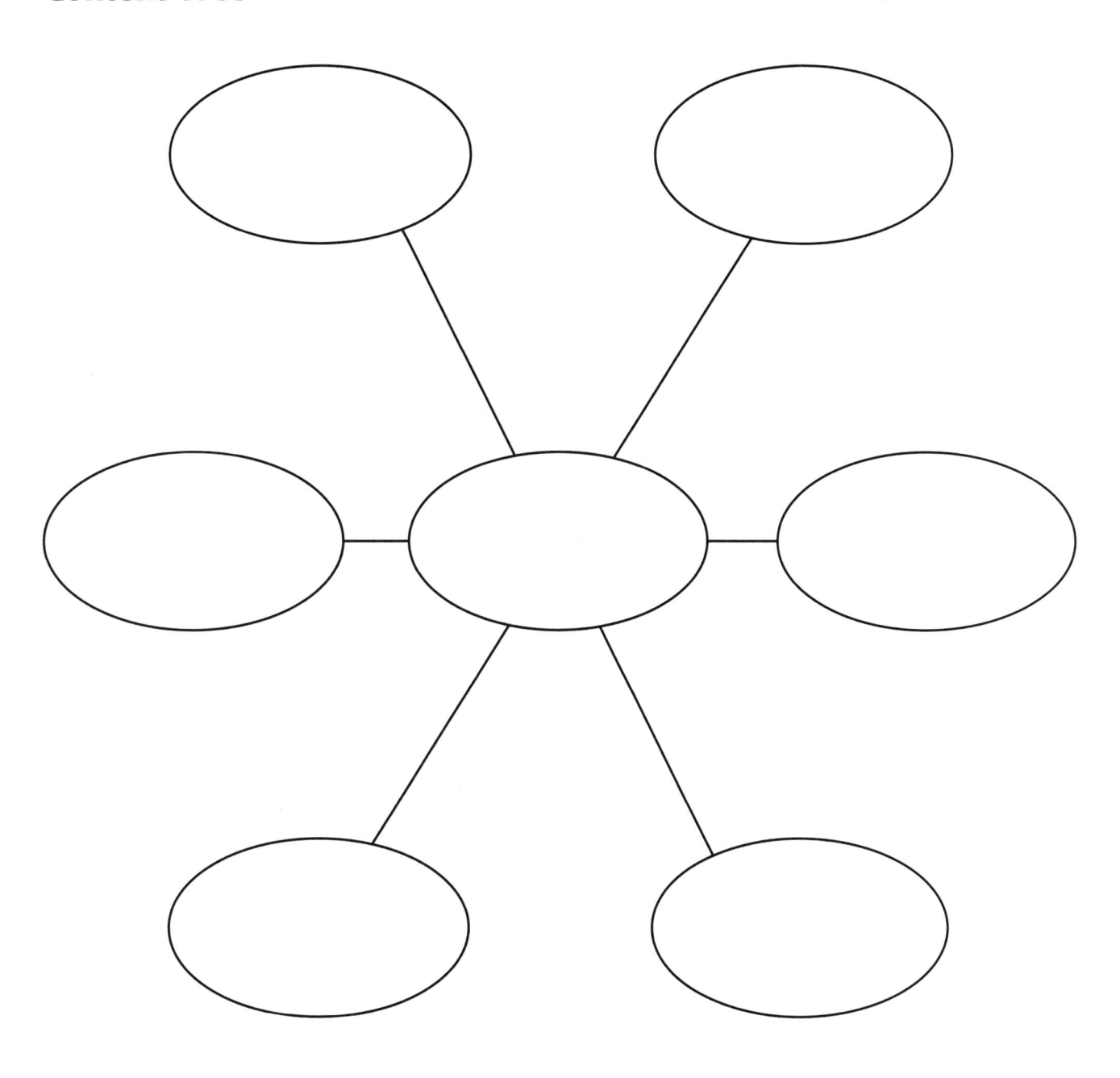

Discovery 113

Graphic Organizer

Name _____ Date _____

The Prince and the Beggar
Compare and Contrast Diagram

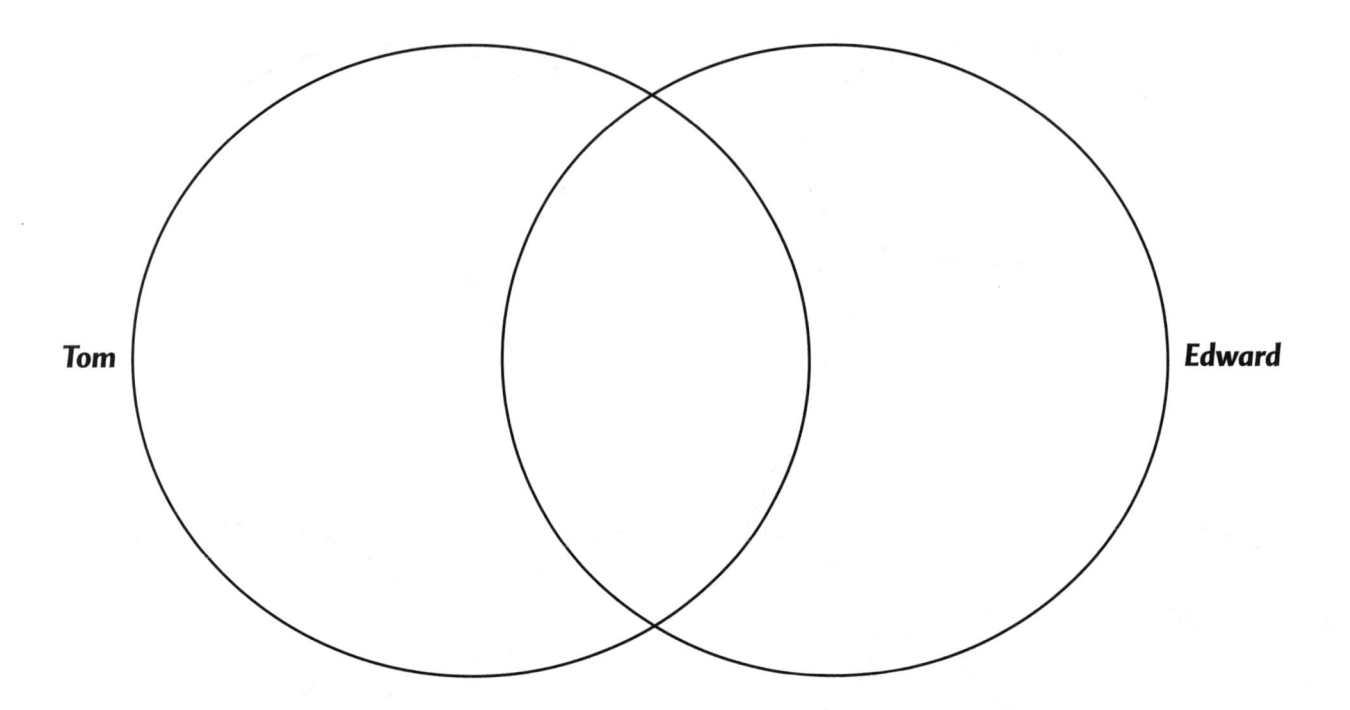

Tom   Edward

- What is **different** about Tom goes in the circle on the left.
- What is **different** about Edward goes in the circle on the right.
- What is the **same about both** goes in the overlapping area in the middle.

Graphic Organizer

Name _____ Date _____

Swiss Family Robinson
Book Report Form

On lines 1–4, list the major plot events. On line 5, write the turning point or climax of the conflict. On line 6, write the falling action. On line 7, write how the story ended.

1. _____

2. _____

3. _____

4. _____

Rising Action

Climax

5. _____

Falling Action

6. _____

7. _____

Resolution

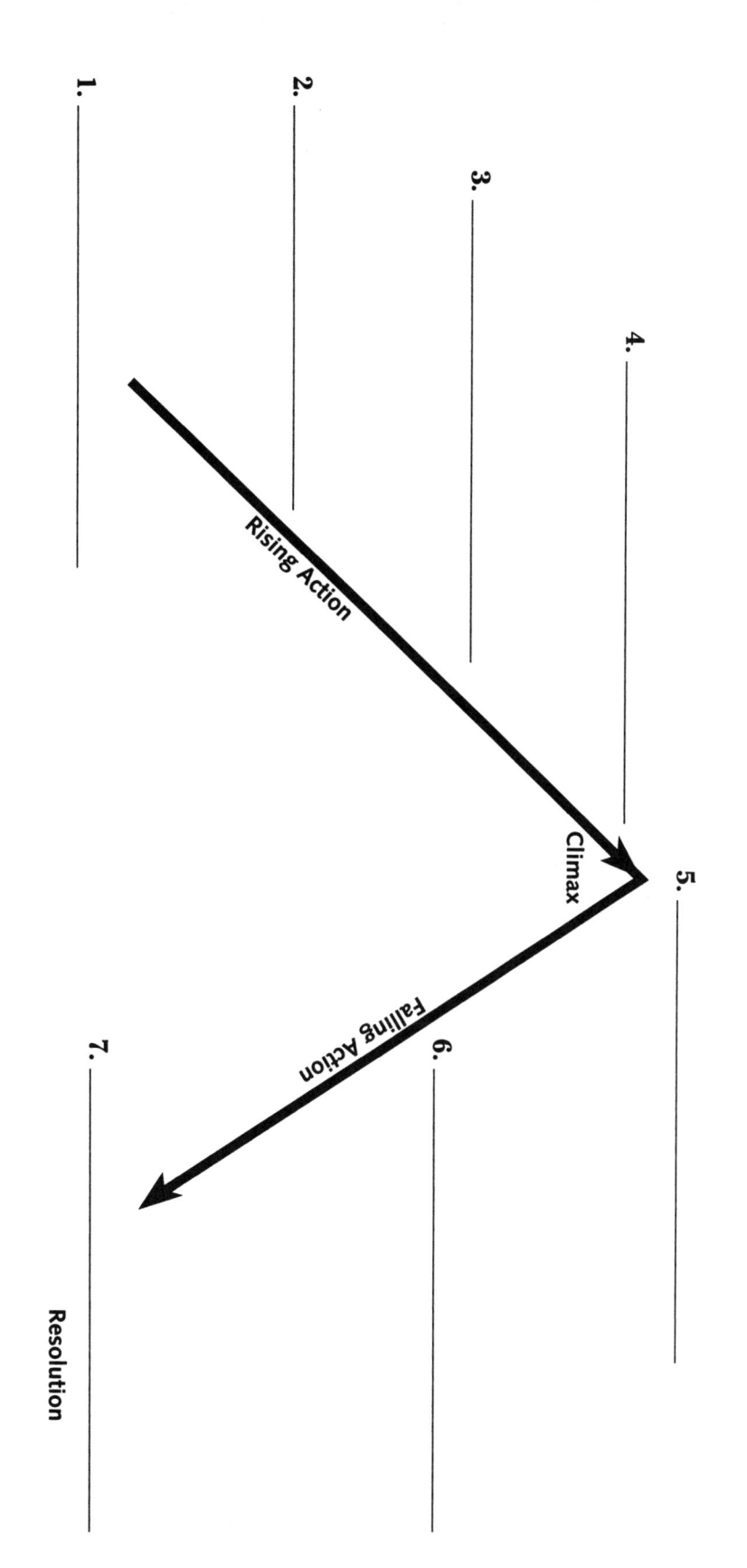

Discovery